Owned

the society pages

the
society
pages

owned

douglas hartmann
UNIVERSITY OF MINNESOTA

christopher uggen
UNIVERSITY OF MINNESOTA

w. w. norton & company
NEW YORK | LONDON

W. W. Norton & Company has been independent since its founding in 1923, when William Warder Norton and Mary D. Herter Norton first published lectures delivered at the People's Institute, the adult education division of New York City's Cooper Union. The firm soon expanded its program beyond the Institute, publishing books by celebrated academics from America and abroad. By mid-century, the two major pillars of Norton's publishing program—trade books and college texts—were firmly established. In the 1950s, the Norton family transferred control of the company to its employees, and today—with a staff of four hundred and a comparable number of trade, college, and professional titles published each year—W. W. Norton & Company stands as the largest and oldest publishing house owned wholly by its employees.

Book Design: Isaac Tobin
Composition: Westchester Book Composition
Manufacturing: Courier-Westford
Production Manager: Sean Mintus

ISBN: 978-0-393-92040-6

W. W. Norton & Company, Inc., 500 Fifth Avenue, New York, NY 10110-0017
www.wwnorton.com
W. W. Norton & Company, Ltd., Castle House, 75/76 Wells Street, London
W1T3QT

thesocietypages.org

contents

series preface

DOUGLAS HARTMANN AND CHRISTOPHER UGGEN

t started with a conversation about record labels. Our favorite imprints are known for impeccable taste, creative design, and an eye for both quality and originality. They consistently deliver the best work by the most original voices. Wouldn't it be cool if W. W. Norton & Company and TheSocietyPages.org joined forces to develop a book series with the same goals in mind?

The Society Pages (TSP) is a multidisciplinary online hub bringing fresh social scientific knowledge and insight to the broadest public audiences in the most open, accessible, and timely manner possible. The largest, most visible collection of sociological material on the web (currently drawing about a million hits per month), TSP is composed of a family of prolific blogs and bloggers, podcasts, features, teaching content, and ongoing research spotlights like There's Research on That!,

Citings & Sitings, and the Reading List. The TSP book series, published in collaboration with W. W. Norton, assembles the best original content from the website in key thematic collections. With contributions from leading scholars and a provocative collection of discussion topics and group activities, this innovative series provides an accessible and affordable entry point for strong sociological perspectives on topics of immediate social import and public relevance.

Volume 4 of our series addresses the new social science of debt. As in our previous volumes, the chapters are organized into three main sections. "Core Contributions" show how sociologists and other social scientists make sense of phenomena like student loans and court fees. Chapters in the "Cultural Contexts" section engage debt through cultural realms—ranging from Detroit's crumbling infrastructure to global climate debt—that are often ignored or taken for granted. Finally, the "Critical Takes" chapters provide sociological commentary and reflection on credit, debt, and the American dream.

Each of these concise, accessible chapters reflects TSP's distinctive layout, tone, and style. Sprinkled throughout are short "TSP Tie-Ins," highlighting new and emerging work on the website and in the field. And the volume concludes with a Discussion Guide and Group Activities section that challenges readers to draw connections among the chapters, think more deeply and critically about debt in social life, and link to ongoing conversations and interactive posts online.

introduction

DOUGLAS HARTMANN AND CHRISTOPHER UGGEN

"Every school offers financial aid services, but listen to what the University of Minnesota is doing," began Michelle Obama at a 2014 White House summit. "They're committing to expand those services to include financial literacy programs to help students and their families manage the costs of college."

In fact, all incoming students at the U of M now get lessons in credit and debt as part of the "Live Like a Student Now So You Don't Have to Later" campaign. The website, Facebook page, and campus posters offer a steady stream of practical advice on everything from buying generic ketchup to finding the free days at local museums. A page titled "Plan Your Debt" even suggests the maximum advisable debt limit for students planning careers as graphic designers, nurses, and accountants.

Such programs can be a great help to individual students, but they also obscure a bigger sociological story: structural and institutional changes place young people today at risk of enormous debt loads. When Chris started college at the University of Wisconsin in the early 1980s, the annual tuition was only $994 per year ($2,442 in today's dollars), which barely covers a course these days. So, it hardly seems fair to blame today's freshmen for accumulating more debt than we did—or to blame their debt problems on $4 lattes. As you'll see in this volume, sociology helps us gain a clear understanding of shifts in resource flows, outlines structural critiques, and even shows us ways forward.

In C. Wright Mills's famous terms, the sociological imagination reveals the link between our "personal troubles" with debt and the broader "public issues" that have placed us in this position. And it isn't just students. For the past five years, headlines have shouted about all manner of debt—people, companies, and even cities declaring bankruptcy, families losing their homes to foreclosure, and the Occupy Wall Street movement arising to challenge the "1%" who prospered in the Great Recession.

Learning about these structural problems can be dispiriting, which is why we sometimes call sociology the "Debbie Downer" of the social sciences. But understanding the structural forces that shape our lives is also empowering—likely even more empowering than the personal finance curriculum praised by Michelle Obama (who did, after all, major in sociology).

In our TSP series, we select pieces that show how a distinctively sociological orientation differs from that of other approaches, particularly those of economics, the scholarly discipline most closely associated with credit and debt. In curating the site and reviewing and editing these submissions, we learned a lot about the power and importance of a sociological approach to debt and inequality. A great strength of this volume is that it collects up-to-the-minute essays from an area in which both public debate and the research literature are exploding. Taken together, the chapters provide a useful entrée to a rapidly developing area—what we call a "new sociology of debt and inequality."

section-by-section organization

Owned is organized in three main sections, each of which highlights distinctive aspects of the sociological vision of and approach to debt.

CORE CONTRIBUTIONS

Whenever political stakes are high, the basic social facts can be hotly contested. So we asked a real expert, Kevin Leicht, to kick us off by explaining the development and depth of the debt crisis. With hard data and vivid description, he shows how middle-class families suffer when borrowing replaces earning. Next, we really wanted to dig into the debt problem for young people. In "Out of the Nest and into the Red," Jason Houle shows *exactly* how debt has shifted across the last three generations. The third chapter takes up the financial obligations that our criminal justice system imposes. Alexes Harris, the innovative scholar who introduced the subject to sociology, shows how these sanctions work, why debt is so often a life sentence, and the practical steps needed for reform. But we couldn't leave the core contributions section without directly engaging the racial dimensions of the debt crisis. The distinguished scholars in our roundtable— Dalton Conley, Rachel Dwyer, and Karyn Lacy—detail the challenges facing minority borrowers, who often have little access to the "good" debt that builds wealth. Finally, in his tie-in on the subjective experience of debt, Rahsaan Mahadeo introduces three path-breaking studies of the morality and social experience of debt.

CULTURAL CONTEXTS

These chapters engage debt and inequality across diverse cultural realms. Robert Crosnoe shows that we can't understand today's extreme educational inequalities without looking to the home. He makes a convincing case that our efforts to help kids depend on how we support their parents and argues for a two-generation, "side-by-side" strategy. David Schalliol is a professional photographer as well as a sociologist, and his eye for the telling detail is apparent in "Debt and Darkness in Detroit." The burnt-out city streetlights represent both a reflection of the city's bankruptcy and a vexing challenge to its social and economic recovery. Next, Erin Hoekstra's provocative interview with Andrew Ross discusses debtors' movements like the Rolling Jubilee project, which uses crowdfunding to buy up personal debt in a "bailout of the people by the people." In "Of Carbon and Cash," Hoekstra then broadens the picture to global debt and reparations, raising intriguing questions about the morality of debt and who should pay for environmental damage: today's big polluters like China or long-term polluters like the United States?

CRITICAL TAKES

In truth, there's a critical edge to each of the chapters in *Owned.* But while sociologists are documenting the many ways debt has exacerbated inequalities and social problems, they are also imagining alternatives. What can and should we do to change the situation? Leicht offers a hard-hitting, progressive critique of the "politics of displacement" that distract us from needed economic reform, while proposing three steps to reinvigorate the American dream. Next, Eric Best tackles the for-profit education industry, which threatens to produce a glut of unmarketable degrees and unpayable student debt. He concludes that the fix will be expensive, since the largest for-profit educators are both "too big to fail and too big to succeed." Perhaps there are other routes to reform: G. William Domhoff, the dean of American inequality scholars and author of all-time classics like *Who Rules America?*, considers whether worker control of pension funds could help level the playing field. In "Pension Fund Capitalism," he shows why the institutional investor's movement has had little impact on corporate power. And Leicht returns for the last word in the volume, contrasting the old "pull yourself up by your bootstraps" success narrative with the current structural realities. As he concludes, the debt crisis is a social problem that cries out for society-level solutions, rather than individual-level admonitions.

The best sociology has long been critical of existing social arrangements and idealistic about the alternatives. The new sociology of debt is no exception. In detailing the grand society-level problems of the debt crisis, the authors in *Owned* point to social solutions on scales both ginormous (global climate reparations) and modest (a lone shopkeeper lighting his street). And making small reforms to alleviate human suffering is hardly incompatible with changing the structural conditions that create or sustain the problem. Students can simultaneously rally for lower tuition and loan rates for everyone as they learn about personal finance to manage their own debt. Some might dismiss the latter efforts as "Band-Aids" for the structural issues, but we wouldn't discount them completely. A well-applied Band-Aid can sometimes stop the bleeding while we pursue a more lasting fix to our problems.

changing lenses: debt, foreclosure, and a little help from your friends

DOUGLAS HARTMANN WITH WING YOUNG HUIE

When I told Wing Young Huie that we were putting together a volume on debt, he couldn't immediately think of any images from his portfolio that would capture the theme. He'd photographed rundown places, sure, but debt was a different story than poverty. Then he had me take a look at this picture from his "We Are the Other" project.

The photo shows two men, Bobby and Reggie, sitting in a kitchen. Save for the fact that the men are of different races, as well as the haunting self-consciousness of the unnamed man on the right, I didn't immediately understand the significance of this image, let alone its relation to debt. It could be a photo of a neighborly chat, a family gathering, or a work break. But then Wing shared the story behind the image.

© Wing Young Huie, reprinted with permission.

The kitchen is Bobby's and his house is just down the street from Wing's in South Minneapolis. One of nine children, Bobby has lived in the same house since his mother bought it in 1968. On February 17, 2012, Bobby's house was the center of a block party called the "Foreclosure Free Fest." Turns out that Bobby, a proud 57-year-old plasterer

changing lenses: debt, foreclosure, and a little help

and former Marine, had fallen behind on his mortgage after a series of health problems. This picture was taken that evening.

The event drew 300 supporters throughout the night, with a lineup of well-known local musicians who performed in Bobby's small living room and on a stage on his front lawn. Bobby didn't know everyone who came that night, but one person he did know was Reggie. They grew up together in South Minneapolis and met in the seventh grade. "We ran the neighborhood," says Bobby. "We fought each other and fought everyone else. But that's the way it was, you beat someone up, and they end up your best friend."

With coverage from ABC News and the Huffington Post, as well as the support of his friends, neighbors, and those in the Occupy movement, Bobby was able to get Bank of America to offer a mortgage modification that allowed him to keep his home. The support seems miraculous to Bobby: "It's like I fell in the mud and can now come up for clean air all the time."

Bobby is, of course, one of thousands, even millions, of Americans struggling with debt and foreclosure—each one with a story, each one with some friends and neighbors and support, and yet they have little media coverage that can lead to real assistance as they struggle to maintain the piece of the American dream they thought they'd already achieved.

core contributions

has borrowing replaced earning?

KEVIN LEICHT

Since the 1980s, corporate profits have reached record levels, while the earnings and incomes of the middle class have stagnated or dropped. Yet, as former U.S. labor secretary Robert Reich and others point out, 80% of the American economy is driven by consumption spending. This means corporate profits are tied to consumption. But if wages and incomes have stagnated, what's been driving the economy? Easily available consumer credit!

The recent relationship among consumption, credit, and profits has severed the "virtuous cycle" among rising earnings, consumption, and profits that drove the U.S. economy from the end of World War II to the mid-1970s. In this cycle, consumption was driven by workers' earnings, which rose steadily as the economy grew. Increases in wages fueled more consumption, which fueled more profits, more investment, higher wages, and still more consumption. In this environment, it wasn't possible for profits to rise in the suites without earnings rising on the streets.

But then something changed. As Scott Fitzgerald and I argue in *Postindustrial Peasants: The Illusion of Middle-Class Prosperity* and *Middle Class Meltdown in America: Causes, Consequences, and Remedies*, borrowing replaced earning as the major driver of consumer spending. This was made possible by the deregulation of financial markets and the lowering of credit and lending standards. The result was the 2008 financial markets crash, when investors and speculators lost confidence in the ability of people and corporations to make good on their debts.

The pre-2008 recession ties among consumption, credit, and profits has led us to question claims that things were peachy before and economic prosperity is just around the corner again. In the United States, we have spent a great deal of time making life better for those who are already relatively wealthy. We've also harmed the economic prospects of everyone else. Middle-class families, whose main source of income is employment and main source of wealth is an owner-occupied home, have been losing big-time. And their losses have been mounting for years. Easily available credit has essentially covered up these losses by boosting the spending power of those whose earning power was on the decline. Looking at the statistics, the path we've trod is pretty clear: Since the late 1970s, the U.S. middle class has experienced an unprecedented decline in real purchasing power. The productivity gains of the 1980s and '90s were not reflected in the average worker's paycheck. Wages slid against inflation. Gaps between stagnant incomes and consumption aspirations were filled by easily available credit. Simultaneously, the deregulation of credit and financial markets that created many ways to lend money externalized the risk of bad loans through such unwieldy tools as "asset-backed securities" and "collateralized debt obligations." Market risk was shifted from banks to the rest of us.

The 2008 recession ended the era of easy credit.

The middle class became, as Fitzgerald and I put it, a class of "postindustrial peasants." Debt made the labor of middle-class workers look more like the serfdom of agrarian economies than the skilled work of modern citizens.

profits up, wages . . .

The evidence that profits have risen while wages and earnings have not is clear. While corporate profits and incomes for the wealthiest tenth of taxpayers have risen steadily, median pretax family income has barely moved, rising less than 20% in real dollars since 1971. Wages among those already well-off (that top 10% of the earnings distribution

Median Before-Tax Family Income, 1971–2012

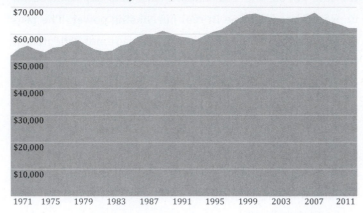

Source: U.S. Census Bureau, Current Population Survey, Annual Social and Economic Supplements.
Notes: 2012 dollars.
Graphic created for TheSocietyPages.org by Suzy McElrath

Workers' Hourly Wages as a Percentage of 1973 Hourly Wages by Percentile, 1973–2012

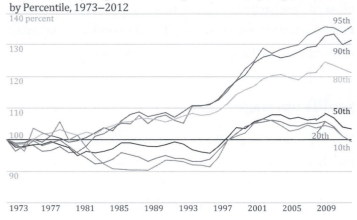

Source: Economic Policy Analysis, The State of Working America, 12th edition.
Notes: Real hourly wages for all workers as a percentage of 1973 real hourly wages, 2012 dollars.
Graphic created for TheSocietyPages.org by Suzy McElrath

mentioned above) have ballooned since the 1970s, while wages of the bottom 50% have barely moved at all. Further, according to the Economic Policy Institute, CEO compensation has increased 875% since 1978. Back then, the CEO-to-worker pay ratio was 29 to 1; by 2012, it was 273 to 1.

In these years when wages were going nowhere, U.S. citizens were borrowing money (lots of it) and the savings rate effectively hit nothing by 2006 (the shaded areas on the chart below show the years in which the economy was in recession). If the average American's wages had risen along with productivity gains, the real median 1992 wage

U.S. Net Savings as a Percentage of Gross National Income, 1970–2013

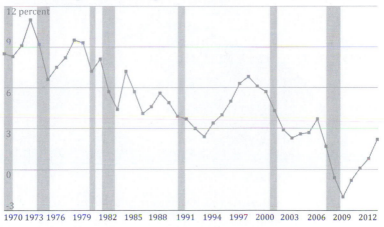

Source: U.S. Bureau of Economic Analysis, National Income and Products Accounts, Table 5.1.
Graphic created for TheSocietyPages.org by Suzy McElrath

of $11.37 an hour would have risen to $19.15 today, rather than the real amount: $16.87 an hour. And $23,600 in 1992 would have translated into $34,300 in 2006. Since this change would have been in real dollars, the median wage earner would have seen his or her purchasing power increase by over a third, instead of just $800. That's a lot of potential income going *somewhere else* for *some other* reason.

Over the long term, it really does appear that the middle class replaced the purchasing power of nonexistent raises with easily available credit. The type of indentured servitude social scientists such as Juliet Schorr, Jacob Hacker,

Average U.S. Credit Card Debt Per Household, 1990-2012

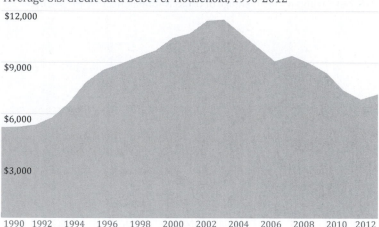

Notes: Data for 2004 and 2005 are linearly interpolated. 2012 dollars.
Graphic created for TheSocietyPages.org by Suzy McElrath

Dalton Conley, and others have discussed means many citizens end up slaves to their debts, working more hours for less money (working hours have risen by 40% in the last 30 years), sending both spouses into the labor market, and remaining stuck in a cycle of "spend, work, and pay debt." With big debts, no savings, and no more laborers to add to the workforce, the great majority of families are only one missed paycheck away from defaulting on their bills. Then, in 2008, easy consumer credit dried up. With credit now hard to obtain, the same families face large debts, small or missing paychecks, and creditors knocking on their doors.

credit then and now

Many readers under 30 probably don't remember the credit markets in place as recently as the mid-1980s. You had to apply for a credit card (usually from a bank). You had to prove that you had a job and report your income and any outstanding debts. If you were under 21, your parents had to cosign the credit card application—essentially ensuring that if you did not pay back the debt, they would (and the card would have a low spending limit). The bank would look at your application, decide whether you were a good credit risk, and then set a limit on your credit card spending. If you came anywhere near the spending limit, the card was usually canceled. You could no longer borrow until your debt was paid down.

The same was true with auto and home loans. Applications were long and tedious, and there was little or no "instant credit." Minimum down payments ranged between 10 and 20% of the full price of the car or house, and the bank or credit union spent a great deal of time evaluating your creditworthiness and whether you could afford the loan payments. Most interest rates were fixed (rather than variable) and they usually weren't low (my first car loan came with a 17.5% interest rate in 1981; my first mortgage interest rate was 11.5% in 1990—two to three times today's interest rates).

The deregulation of financial markets changed all of that. Big banks consolidated, and new lenders of all kinds started to sprout up to finance mortgages and auto loans. These new lenders were not subject to the same regulations as banks. Many bank regulations were loosened, such as restrictions on interest rates and fees, and limits on interstate banking and the consolidation of bank assets. Loan terms eased considerably, and the creation of the asset-backed securities market meant that many loan originators didn't even hold on to their outstanding loans—they sold the loans and their risk to securities firms that, in turn, sold the outstanding debt to investors willing to bet on riskier loans. That is, investors now took the risk that you might *not* be able to pay back your loan.

lured into a cycle of debt

Ironically, financial deregulation hit right as the squeeze of wage stagnation and job instability was most acute—the late 1980s to mid-1990s. Middle-class purchasing power was headed nowhere when people started to get tempting credit card offers in the mail. "No proof of income necessary!" "Instant credit!" Suddenly you could drive a new car off the lot with no down payment or you could lease rather than buy it (returning the asset once the lease was up—essentially a long-term car rental). And for mortgages, many of the traditional loan-eligibility restrictions were lifted, setting off an artificially inflated "housing boom" driven by easy credit and borrowed money.

In extreme cases, home loans came with several introductory "teaser" interest rates. In the early portions of the loan term, individuals might only pay the interest accrued in each period, ending up owing more each month if they only paid the minimum. Often, the teaser rates readjusted to higher, fixed interest rates after just a few years.

None of this has been helped by the serious and often hidden inflation affecting goods and services the middle class has come to rely on. As Elizabeth Warren and Amelia Tyagi pointed out in *The Two-Income Trap: Why Middle-Class Parents Are Going Broke*, home prices in good neighborhoods have gone up 214% in the past 20 years. These good neighborhoods are "good" because they have good schools in them, and parents increasingly use two incomes as ammunition in the competition to buy a home in a good school district. But once they've secured this home, an interesting economic dance of deception is put in motion. Since jobs aren't as steady as they once were and earnings don't rise as they once did, that good home in that good neighborhood is a few missed paychecks away from foreclosure. But the deregulated credit market gives couples an array of options to try to "keep" the house while they try to secure more income: They can take out a second mortgage, raid retirement and college funds, and put mortgage payments on credit cards. (In the rarer and rarer cases in which a couple has paid off their home, they can ease the pain of constricted retirement funds and Social Security payments by taking out a "reverse mortgage"; they will now be paid monthly for their home, slowly giving it away to an investor and hoping they won't outlive the loan term.)

What else is getting more terrifyingly expensive? Well, we've allowed the cost of state-supported higher education to rise much faster than inflation. College is now a private good paid for by student loans, not a public good consistently supported by states. As any small business owner will tell you, employer-provided health insurance is also becoming unaffordable, not only because employers are socked with big increases every year but also because the payments expected of employees rise every year. While implementation of the Affordable Care Act will likely increase coverage, social scientists must begin asking more complicated questions about employer-provided health insurance. Today, many employees don't take the coverage their employer provides because they simply can't afford it. And then there's child care: The average annual outlay for child care in the United States is now almost $11,666 per child. That average of $972 per month per child is beyond the reach of all but the most secure members of the upper middle class, but high-quality child care is a key factor in strong school starts and the development of the cognitive and social skills needed to succeed as adults. That's a tough choice.

Meanwhile, the classic "defined-benefit" pension is almost gone. Stable retirement plans that guaranteed a minimum payout based on investments of company money and employee contributions have been replaced by 401(k) and other "defined-contribution" plans. These plans create more uncertainty for millions of people, whose finances in retirement are dependent on their own savings and the performance of a financial market that many do not fully understand. This is not a formula for success at any level.

child care

the new virtuous cycle

Record profits for corporations in the last decade have been produced almost entirely by lending money to middle-class consumers while letting their wages slide. The virtuous cycle connecting profits to the purchasing power created by jobs and earnings was severed—now all one needed to do was loan money to consumers (or get someone else to do it) and profits would follow (without the corresponding wages and job security once required of employers). The virtuous cycle that Robert Reich talks about has been recreated, but in a perverse form. Only the top 1%, whose incomes are derived from profits, dividends, and property ownership, can get in on the virtuous cycle and avoid the debt cycle.

The Obama administration and its successors face a fairly unpalatable set of choices. The easiest is to simply turn the credit spigot back on, allow the securities aftermarket to spread the risks, and pray that there isn't another crisis of confidence in the financial markets. That's the easy road, but it will surely lead to more inequality and downward mobility. It would retain the trappings of middle-class status (houses, cars, vacations, and college educations) and the profits of companies.

The harder choice involves creating an alternate narrative that recognizes that family values cost money; that those who make a killing in financial markets should have to share profits with others; that the decision whether to invest, save, and work shouldn't be distorted by a tax system that favors unearned over earned income; and that lenders must be held accountable for the credit they advance to consumers. That alternative seems both idealistic and unattainable, but it's neither. It is the type of realistic change that middle-class citizens should demand.

RECOMMENDED READING

Jacob S. Hacker and Paul Pierson. 2010. *Winner-Take-All Politics: How Washington Made the Rich Richer—and Turned Its Back on the Middle Class,* New York: Simon & Schuster. Tells the story of how American politics created today's enormous economic inequalities.

Kevin T. Leicht and Scott T. Fitzgerald. 2007. *Postindustrial Peasants: The Illusion of Middle-Class Prosperity,* New York: Worth Publishers. Documents the recent struggles of the American middle class, drawing connections with peasants in feudal societies and sharecroppers in agrarian societies.

Lawrence Mishel and Natalie Sabadish. 2013. *CEO Pay in 2012 Was Extraordinarily High Relative to Typical Workers and Other High Earners,* Washington, DC: Economic Policy Institute. A comprehensive report on trends in the compensation of top executives.

Juliet B. Schor. 1998. *The Overspent American: Why We Want What We Don't Need,* New York: Basic Books. A critical analysis of American consumer culture.

Elizabeth Warren and Amelia Warren Tyagi. 2004. *The Two-Income Trap: Why Middle-Class Parents Are Going Broke,* New York: Basic Books. Explains how two-income families are increasingly trapped by economic forces.

out of the nest and into the red

JASON N. HOULE

the dynamics of debt in young adulthood

In any newspaper or blog these days, you're bound to find human interest stories of fresh-faced young adults, newly independent from their parents and saddled by a mountain of debt they can't even dream of repaying. The media narrative—think the white college student plagued by $120,000 of student loan and credit card debt—often borders on hyperbole. It skews the reality of how much debt the typical young adult owes.

And while youth indebtedness has received rampant media coverage, there's been very little solid research tackling this emerging social problem. Evidence from a small group of researchers examining how youth debt has changed over time, how youth indebtedness is linked to social stratification and inequality, and the consequences of debt for young people as they advance through their adult lives can give us a glimpse. The research in this area is nascent, and some of it is contradictory, in large part because access to credit and debt carries an array of costs and benefits and is influenced by social and structural factors, such as race, class, and education. Debt can surely open doors and create access, but it can also close doors by imposing a long-term burden on debtors and their families.

three generations of debt

Over the past 50 years, the period known as the "transition to adulthood" has changed dramatically. In the 1960s and '70s, young people left the parental home, completed education, got married, and had children in a relatively quick and orderly fashion. Today's transition to adulthood is much more complex. Young people are extending their education and delaying marriage and childbearing, and some are returning to live with relatives. They enter and exit college, cohabitate rather than marry, and take longer periods for "self-discovery" if they are able. While youth must now navigate this increasingly complex transition, they also take on unprecedented financial risk. Whether it's the result of pursuing a college degree, getting married, buying a home, or simply paying bills, young adults often assume a great deal of debt as they leave the nest and set out on their own.

The rise of debt in young adulthood has been driven by a potent mix of policy changes, rising costs, and stagnating incomes. On the supply side, young adults have come of age in an era of easy access to credit. Financial deregulation in the 1970s and '80s increased the supply of credit and made debt an extremely profitable business for banks. It was aggressively marketed toward consumers—particularly young adults—which led to a massive increase in household debt and problems with repayment. On the demand side, rising costs—such as the skyrocketing price of college—make credit an appealing option. Since their parents already have debt, young people must take on debt of their own.

In a recent study for *Social Problems,* I used data from the National Longitudinal Surveys to show how debt has changed across three generations (what we demographers refer to as "cohorts") of young adults. I focused on people in their mid-twenties: the early baby boomers, who were young adults in the late 1970s; the late baby boomers, who were young adults in the late 1980s; and generation Y, who are currently in their twenties.

The following graphic confirms what most laypersons and media reports have suggested: Debt has risen. I show mean and median total debt across three cohorts of young adults, adjusted for inflation and basic sociodemographic factors such as socioeconomic status, race, and age. Total debt is the sum of everything from home mortgages, credit cards, and student loans to automobiles and personal loans. Comparing mean and median debt across cohorts, we notice the mean has increased much faster than the median. While the median gives us a good sense of debt in the middle of the distribution, the mean is far more sensitive to extremely high and extremely low debt loads. What this reveals is that much of the growth in debt across cohorts is being driven by an increase in the number of *severely* indebted young adults. In some ways, it seems the media imagery of the young person beleaguered by extremely high levels of debt is more commonplace today than it was 30 years ago.

Total Debt Across Three Cohorts of Adults

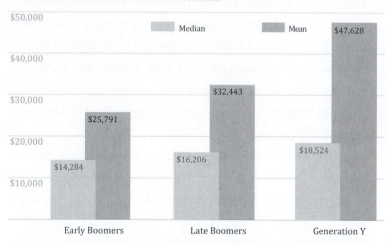

Notes: Estimates adjusted for sociodemographic covariates and weighted for survey design effects.
Source: National Longitudinal Surveys (NLS66/68; NLSY-79; NLSY97).
Graphic created for TheSocietyPages.org by Suzy McElrath

A focus on total debt, however, obscures how difficult it is for youth to actually repay what they've borrowed. For example, we may not be concerned about rising debt if the means to pay down that debt were rising at the same pace. In the figure below, I show two standard measures of debt burden, or debt relative to economic resources, that indicate how difficult it is for young people to pay off debt. Debt relative to assets (debt-to-asset ratio) and debt relative to income (non-mortgage debt-to-income ratio) has increased considerably across the three cohorts. The debt-to-asset ratio is particularly high for generation Y, suggesting that the median young adult household would have to liquidate

Median Debt Burden Across Three Cohorts of Young Adults

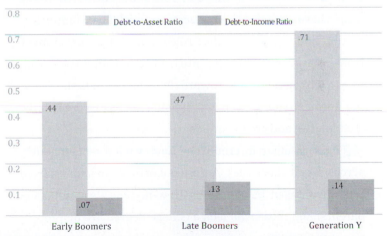

Notes: Estimates adjusted for sociodemographic covariates and weighted for survey design effects.
Source: National Longitudinal Surveys (NLS66/68; NLSY-79; NLSY97).
Graphic created for TheSocietyPages.org by Suzy McElrath

71% of its assets to pay off its outstanding debts. In addition to facing higher amounts of debt than the cohorts that came before, the generation Y cohort is more likely to be trapped in debt.

While indebtedness and debt burdens generally increased across cohorts, so too did the types of debt young adults take on. My final figure shows how credit use in young adulthood has changed. For the early boomers, home mortgage debt dominated. Across cohorts, student loan debt has replaced home mortgage debt as the primary form of wealth-building debt. Credit card debt has also become a more visible part of the household balance sheet. In some ways, these changes in credit use across cohorts reflect the broader structural shifts in the transition to adulthood I wrote about earlier. As young people have extended their education and delayed family formation and entry into adult roles, they have moved away from debt that signals entry into traditional adult roles, such as home ownership, and toward debt that signals the evolving needs of young people and rising access to credit, like student loan and credit card debt.

These changes in credit use have varied tremendously across social class lines. Across cohorts, young adults from less advantaged backgrounds (low-income, less educated parents) and those who lack a college degree are disproportionately taking on unsecured debt (the kind that isn't tied to

Credit Use and Debt Portfolios Across Three Cohorts of Young Adults

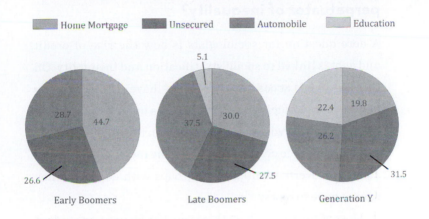

Notes: Estimates adjusted for sociodemographic covariates and weighted for survey design effects.
Source: National Longitudinal Surveys (NLS66/68; NLSY-79; NLSY97).
Graphic created for TheSocietyPages.org by Suzy McElrath

an asset like a house or a car). Meanwhile, across cohorts, college-educated youth and those from more advantaged social class backgrounds have taken on more wealth-building debt, especially education loans. This growing disparity in debt portfolios suggests that, in the latest generation of young adults, the more advantaged are able to take on debt that helps them pursue a middle-class lifestyle and build their wealth, while the less advantaged must take on debt to pay their bills and keep their heads above water. This raises a big question: What is the role of debt in maintaining or alleviating social inequality?

debt: the great equalizer or perpetuator of inequality?

A core question for sociologists is how the rise of credit and debt is linked to social stratification and inequality. On the one hand, access to credit may have afforded many opportunities—such as a new home or a quality education—that would otherwise be out of reach. On the other, debt may serve to reinforce or exacerbate existing inequalities by race and class, overburdening some groups with debt that they cannot hope to repay.

Most of the research on this issue has focused on student loans, which have provided many with access to a college degree. As sociologists have long known, getting a college degree is central to upward social mobility and is, for many, a vital pathway to the American middle class. But because of uneven access to higher education, student loan availability may maintain certain inequalities, affording opportunity for some, but not all, potential students.

For young adults, it isn't yet clear whether student loan *debt* is providing opportunities or reinforcing inequality, though it is clear that debt breaks along social class and racial lines. In a recent study in *Sociology of Education*, I found that parents' education, income, and race are strongly predictive of the amount of student loan debt acquired by young adults who attend postsecondary institutions. Specifically, young adults from lower-middle-income and less educated backgrounds have a significantly higher risk of carrying student loan debt in young adulthood than their more affluent counterparts. Moreover, African Americans have considerably more debt in young adulthood than their white counterparts, which may reflect the overarching legacy of disadvantages faced by African Americans. When we consider that young adults with excessive debt are at a greater risk for dropping out of college, defaulting on their loans, and entering bankruptcy, student loan debt looks more like a perpetuator than a panacea for inequality.

On the flip side, some research suggests that, at modest levels, student loan debt could help alleviate educational inequalities. For example, low levels of student loan debt—up to $10,000—actually reduce the risk of college dropout. Perhaps that number is about enough debt to make staying in college seem worth it, but not so much that the student feels hopeless before ever getting to graduation. Related research shows that, despite the fact that black students have higher levels of student loan debt than whites, debt increases enrollment and persistence in college among African Americans. However, this same work shows that high levels of student loan debt ($15,000 or more) can increase the risk of dropping out of college. While debt may increase college access, as some young people take on more debt they begin to feel over-burdened and many leave without a degree.

Indeed, more and more students *do* leave college with debt but no degree. This shows how going to college is a greater gamble for young people today than it was in the past. In the 1960s, those who dropped out of college had little or no debt and could enter a strong labor market with access to decent-paying middle-class jobs. Today, those who leave college without a degree are largely unable to acquire middle-class jobs and may feel doomed to their debt. Indeed, in Katherine Porter's groundbreaking study on middle-class bankruptcy, she found that student loan debtors who drop out are at par-ticularly high risk of declaring bankruptcy since they strug-gle both to make ends meet and keep up with loan payments. This is in spite of the fact that bankruptcy does not discharge education debt. A recent report in the *Chronicle of Higher Education* demonstrates that bind: Default rates are rising among student loan debtors.

The story of student loan burdens is consistent with the narrative that debt has both costs and benefits for young people—what sociologist Rachel Dwyer and colleagues call a "double-edged sword." It is a borrowed resource that can bridge the gap between rising college costs and lower paren-tal resources, but it can also be difficult to repay, especially for those students who don't finish a degree.

consequences of debt in young adulthood

This idea that debt is a double-edged sword is also apparent in some important new studies on how debt affects young people's economic, social, and psychological well-being. This research suggests that debt's benefits become detriments once payment comes due. For example, Dwyer and colleagues found that having student loans and credit cards led some young people to feel empowered and in greater control of their lives; it offered freedom and possibility. But these effects wore off as young people grew older and started to repay the debt they accrued along the way. Debtors in their mid- to late twenties tended to feel they had less "control over their lives" and lower levels of mastery. Similarly, debt burden is linked to increased anxiety and depression, suggesting that rising debt is undermining the mental health of young people, at least once the bills show up.

The long-term effect of a heavy debt burden spread across a wider swath of young Americans is a big, unanswered question. When we ask young adults if they feel like debt is holding them back, many say it prevented them from going for a job or internship they wanted and made them think twice about getting married, buying a home, or having a child (some of the traditional "markers" of adulthood). The research, however, is mixed on this topic. Looking at earlier cohorts of twentysomethings, scholars have found little evidence that debt impacts choices and well-being. More recent generation Y research by Fenaba Addo, however, shows a shift, suggesting that credit card and student loan debt may be leading young women to favor cohabitation and delay marriage.

In the media, the concern focuses on the constraint of young adults' choices and far-reaching effects on the economy. Some outlets believe student loan debt is slowing down the housing market recovery, as overindebted young people decide not to buy homes or are unable to qualify for home mortgages due to their high debt levels and low credit scores. Again, the actual research is less convincing. For instance, Lawrence Berger and I found that young adults with student loan debt are *somewhat* less likely to purchase a home and purchase less expensive homes than similar young adults without student loans. These differences were quite small, though; it is highly unlikely that student loan debtors are dragging down the housing market or holding back its recovery.

So, while news headlines sometimes paint a hyperbolic picture of young debt, sociological research is beginning to give us a more nuanced view. To participate in society and gain economic independence, many young adults today must take a massive financial risk. It's a gamble—a roll of the dice for their future. For some, this gamble may pay off—that line of credit may help them graduate from college, attain their dream job, and live happy, fulfilling lives. But others will find themselves buried under a mountain of debt with little to show for it and even less hope of repayment. In an era of credit expansion, rising prices, and stagnating wages, debt is now an integral part of social life for young adults, and we can't paint it as "good" or "bad," at least not yet. But it is clear that debt accumulation isn't just about personal or financial irresponsibility, as some would lead us to believe. Instead, the rise in debt is strongly tied to historical, social, and structural factors, and debt among today's young adults mirrors existing class and racial divides. Though it is too soon to know, it may well be that debt will come to play an important role in the maintenance and reproduction of socioeconomic and racial inequalities across generations. The big picture is, perhaps, bleaker than any one sad story.

RECOMMENDED READING

Rachel E. Dwyer, Laura McCloud, and Randy Hodson. 2011. "Youth debt, mastery, and self-esteem: Class-stratified effects of indebtedness on self-concept," *Social Science Research* 40:727–741. Examines the positive and negative effects of debt on the well-being of young adults.

Rachel E. Dwyer, Laura McCloud, and Randy Hodson. 2012. "Debt and Graduation from American Universities," *Social Forces* 90:1133–1155. Investigates how debt accumulation affects the risk of dropping out of college.

Randy Hodson, Rachel E. Dwyer, and Lisa A. Neilson. 2014. "Credit Card Blues: The Middle Class and the Hidden Costs of Easy Credit," *The Sociological Quarterly* 55(2): 315–340. Shows that the onset of the Great Recession and rising debt negatively affected the mental health of young adults.

Jason N. Houle. 2014. "A Generation Indebted? Young Adult Debt across Three Cohorts," *Social Problems* 61(3):448–465. Examines how debt has shifted across three cohorts of young adults in the '70s, '80s, and 2000s.

Brandon A. Jackson and John R. Reynolds. 2013. "The Price of Opportunity: Race, Student Loan Debt, and College Achievement," *Sociological Inquiry* 83:335–368. Examines racial inequalities in debt accumulation, college persistence, and student loan default.

the cruel poverty of monetary sanctions

ALEXES HARRIS

"Do the crime, pay the fine." A little different, right? Many are unaware that when convicted of breaking the law, not only do people "pay" for their crimes by doing time but they are also forced to pay up financially. The costs include court processing, defense attorneys, paperwork, and anything else associated with their incarceration and supervision. In fact, anyone convicted of any type of criminal offense is subject to fiscal penalties or monetary sanctions. (If you have ever paid a traffic ticket, for example, you have paid a monetary sanction.) Further, the base fine of, say, a speeding ticket or even a major criminal conviction is just a small portion of the total cost. There are fines, fees, interest, surcharges, per payment and collection charges, and restitution. Until these debts are paid in full, individuals who have otherwise "done their time" remain under judicial supervision and are subject to court summons, warrants, and even jail stays.

As a result of interest and surcharges that accumulate on these financial penalties, this portion of a person's sentence becomes permanent legal debt, carried for the remainder of their lives. And because so many who are arrested and convicted are poor, unemployed, homeless, or suffer from mental or physical illnesses, the fines just pile up—unable to be erased through bankruptcy—and tie them, indefinitely, to the criminal justice system. For them, debt is a life sentence.

how monetary sanctions work

My research investigates the growth, process, and impact of legal financial obligations. Fines have always been imposed in the American criminal justice system. However, starting in the early 1990s, states began changing laws to dramatically expand the number and types of fees and surcharges they could impose. Each state legislature has now constructed particular statutes to detail the types of monetary sanctions that judges can impose in addition to incarceration for felony convictions. Individual counties then implement their *own* formal (legally prescribed by county code) and informal (decided by local clerk offices) that guide amounts imposed at sentencing hearings as well as the procedures for monitoring and collecting these fees.

A recent study of 15 states by the Brennan Center for Justice (at New York University) found that every state studied imposed fines upon conviction; imposed parole, probation, or other supervision fees; and had laws authorizing the imposition of incarceration fees. In Louisiana, indigent defendants are assessed an up-front fee of $40 for their public defender (mind you—the whole point of a public defender is to provide legal counsel for those who cannot afford it), and, at the time of sentencing, they are assessed an additional $300 fee for the "Judicial Expense Fund." North Carolina has a "cost of justice fee" of $154.50 imposed on *all* felony defendants (the fine isn't contingent upon conviction).

In Washington State, monetary sanctions are called legal financial obligations (LFOs). These sanctions are imposed by judges at sentencing hearings but are monitored by court clerks (nonelected bureaucrats). The mandatory minimum LFO is a $500 victim penalty assessment, a $100 DNA collection fee, and a $200 clerk surcharge. As a result of additional fines and fees added, the average monetary felony sentence (not including restitution for victims) in 2004 totaled just under $1,400—an enormous sum for many desperately poor clients in the criminal justice system. These costs are imposed per felony conviction; so, if someone is convicted of multiple counts or offenses, the fines are multiplied. The initial amount also accumulates dramatically: 12% interest begins accruing from the day of sentencing, and a $100 annual collection surcharge is added to unpaid balances per felony conviction. For example, a defendant with an LFO of $1,347 who makes monthly payments of $100 would pay off their fine in 16 months. Assume, however, that the defendant cannot make a payment. By the end of the *sixth month*, the LFO is now a bit over $1,400. After a year the total debt is over $1,600—for *each* charge.

the costs of sanctions

Remember, legally speaking, monetary sanctions are equivalent to court sentences such as jail or prison time, community service, or probation. Until the legal debt is paid in full (including interest and surcharges), the defendant will remain under court jurisdiction, subject to violations for missed payments. Those with unpaid court debts cannot receive certificates of discharge, seal their records, receive pardons, or request deferred prosecution—legal mechanisms meant to allow those who have completed their sentences to move past their felony conviction to become productive citizens. These tools are essential for applying for a job, renting or purchasing a home, and applying for credit, since employers, landlords, and lenders frequently search applicants' credit and legal backgrounds. Legal debt effectively derails prospects for success after conviction.

There are other consequences for poor felony defendants who enter "deferred sentencing agreements," which are intended to remove convictions from legal records *if* all fines, fees, and other court-imposed obligations are met (e.g., attending drug treatment or performing community service). Poor defendants who meet the court requirements but cannot pay their fines and fees will continue to carry a felony record. Those defendants who *can* afford to pay the monetary sanctions, however, can quickly close the door on their criminal justice experience with a deferred sentencing agreement.

In short, poverty, rather than public safety, determines who remains subject to criminal justice surveillance and sanctioning and to the stigmatizing effects of felony conviction. Legal debt is typically substantial relative to the expected earnings of people with felony convictions, and it is usually long term. In several U.S. jurisdictions, felons are regularly summoned to court and incarcerated for making insufficient or irregular payments toward their monetary sanctions. Debt can put a person back behind bars.

twenty-first century debtors' prisons

My 2015 book *A Pound of Flesh* contrasts the growth of monetary sanctions with the legal protections against incarcerating the poor. The United States did away with debtors' prisons in the 1830s, yet we've been expanding contemporary practices of imprisoning those who cannot pay court-related fiscal penalties. Ironically, in an era when state legislatures have decreased judicial discretion in sentencing to limit disparities, we see unfettered discretion in the imposition of fiscal penalties.

Courts can legally impose jail days when those they convict are assessed as "willfully" not paying (i.e., hiding money, not seeking employment to avoid making payments, or not seeking reasonable support from friends or family). Willful nonpayment constitutes contempt of court, so felons are seen as being sanctioned for contempt, not for their inability to pay. In researching my book, I repeatedly observed judges using their discretion to make assessments of nonpaying legal debtors, deciding they had not been putting forth "enough effort" to raise money. One unemployed homeless man in Washington State was told he should have been begging for money by the side of the road to raise money toward his debt.

Homeless, unemployed, or disabled persons like the man I describe are, in many jurisdictions, ordered to serve 10–60 days for contempt of court. Homeless debtors who have no address at which to receive notices of delinquency for nonpayment are frequently arrested for their failure to appear in court. They can spend several nights in jail awaiting hearings. This process of extreme punishments for nonpayment only worsens the class disparities in criminal justice experiences and outcomes.

worsening inequality

Legal debt is important. It affects *many* people—disproportionately poor people and people of color—and it has pernicious, tenacious consequences. And the U.S. criminal justice system affects more and more people each year: 1 in 37 U.S. adults has spent time in state or federal prisons; more than 700,000 people leave prison each year; and there are an estimated 16.1 million current and former felons in the United States. The debt is accumulating at an unimaginable rate.

Ironically, as a result of mass conviction and incarceration, jurisdictions cannot afford criminal justice costs. They are attempting to transfer these expenses to defendants. Since the vast majority of people who receive felony convictions in the United States have minimal employment and income prospects post-conviction, monetary sanctions deepen existing inequalities. Poor people carry the onerous weight of a criminal record in very different ways and for longer periods of time than those with financial resources and good connections (i.e., people from whom they can borrow money). In effect, because they can't pay their debts, the poor become perpetual subjects of the criminal justice system.

why *we* should care

Law-abiding citizens (or those lucky enough to have never been caught and convicted) should care about this criminal justice practice: It is done in our names. The imposition of legal debt leads people convicted of crimes into further political, social, and economic marginalization. It is unproductive. Monetary sanctions attached to felony convictions are not efficient, effective, or ethical.

This is not an efficient process. Because of the lack of automated court data, we do not know the extent of total debt owed, nor is there much information about the total dollars recouped by state and local jurisdictions. There is no consistency in how courts or jails "code" or keep track of defendants incarcerated purely for nonpayment. Thus, we cannot know how many are jailed or how much is spent on monitoring, arresting, and incarcerating people for nonpayment. Researchers truly cannot calculate the total criminal justice resources consumed in managing legal debtors, collecting outstanding debt, and sanctioning those who have not made payments.

This is not an effective process. In many ways, monetary sanctions impose a barrier to rehabilitation or accountability. Legal debtors I have interviewed were frustrated, angry, and distrustful of a system that imposed financial debt in addition to imprisonment, community stigma, and other consequences. When people cannot pay or when the debt *causes* financial hardship, the sentence becomes self-defeating; many will try to avoid the criminal justice system altogether (they will ignore court summons or avoid police when they know they have warrants). Thus, they are not "held accountable" for their offenses, and they become isolated, frustrated, depressed, and disillusioned. Many defendants will never be able to pay off their legal debt (even when making regular payments), and, hence, their "debt to society" stands. Legal debt also affects successful community reintegration: It stymies housing, employment, stable familial relationships, and the ability to view oneself as a productive adult citizen.

This is not an ethical process. Imposing fiscal debt on already marginalized people who will face further marginalization after release from jail or prison is unjust. They have already been sentenced to a host of penalties: incarceration, community supervision, community service, drug and alcohol treatment, and victim panel classes. Adding monetary sanctions sets people up for failure; we *know* the vast majority will never be able to pay off the debt. Further, this system provides a clear example of how the criminal justice system treats the wealthy and the poor differently. People with money can pay their fines and fees the day they are sentenced, with no future nonpayment penalties. They can seal their cases faster. They can avoid repeated trips to the courthouse to make payments, sit before various judges, or provide monthly updates on their employment and housing circumstances. Because of monetary sanctions, the criminal justice experience is dramatically different for poor defendants. The practice sentences poor people to lives of poverty and punishment and releases the wealthy to freedom.

what needs to be done

Discussions about justice and punishment. Local, state, and national jurisdictions must revisit the place of monetary sanctions in contemporary justice. Such discussions could be used as a framework to discuss the reliance on and appropriate role of monetary sanctions in justice processing. Should we try to reform practices to impose more reasonable sentences (either fiscal or physical) that defendants can realistically fulfill? Is it ethical and prudent to impose sentences we know people will never be able to complete? What are the aims, purposes, and end goals of punishment?

Abolition of non-restitution monetary sanctions. My research leads me to conclude that the most sensible policy is to abolish all non-restitution monetary sanctions for criminal offenses. The vast discretion given to judges and court clerks to impose and monitor legal debt and the ways this discretion has been used to further punish poor debtors troubles social justice advocates for very good reason: We cannot assess the total amounts of outstanding debt at local, state, and national levels, so we cannot challenge the notion that monetary sanctions make financial sense. Yet we know three things: Imposing legal debt is counterproductive to the rehabilitative process, it provides a clear example of differential treatment of the wealthy and poor, and it leads to long-term criminal justice surveillance and sanction.

RECOMMENDED READING

American Civil Liberties Union. 2010. "In for a Penny: The Rise of America's New Debtors' Prisons." New York. Examines the implementation of monetary sanctions in five U.S. states to make the case that, despite having outlawed them, the country does have a contemporary system of debtors' prisons.

Alicia Bannon, Mitali Nagrecha, and Rebekah Diller. 2010. "Criminal Justice Debt: A Barrier to Reentry," Brennan Center for Justice at New York University School of Law. Finds that monetary sanctions are increasing across state courts and details how they create a barrier to community reentry postconviction and rehabilitation.

Alexes Harris. 2015. *A Pound of Flesh: Monetary Sanctions as a Permanent Punishment for Poor People.* New York: Russell

Sage Foundation ASA Rose Series in Sociology. Using Washington State as an example, this book examines the growth of monetary sanctions and their effects on the country's most impoverished citizens.

Alexes Harris, Heather Evans, and Katherine Beckett. 2010. "Drawing Blood from Stones: Monetary Sanctions, Punishment and Inequality in the Contemporary United States," *American Journal of Sociology* 115(6):1753–1799. Uses interview data to examine the social and legal consequences of legal fines and fees.

looking into the racial wealth gap with dalton conley, rachel dwyer, and karyn lacy

ERIN HOEKSTRA

The racial wealth gap is one measure that social scientists use to quantify racial economic inequalities. Wealth is considered a comprehensive measure of economic status, as it takes into account household income and assets, as well as levels of indebtedness. Since wealth is often accumulated over generations, the histories and legacies of slavery, Jim Crow laws, discriminatory housing practices, and institutional racism compound to produce discrepancies in wealth along lines of race. The racial wealth gap between white and black Americans usually hovers around 10 to 1, meaning that white households have about 10 times the wealth of African American households. In times of economic hardship, families with less wealth are hit hardest and the gap widens.

This roundtable examines the importance of racial and economic inequality in the context of the Great Recession. Today's racial wealth gap, our panelists say, has resulted from a combination of factors, including housing and home-ownership, access to credit, predatory lending practices, and historically entrenched inequalities.

Since the end of the Great Recession, a number of reports have documented a growing racial wealth gap, including one from Pew Research asserting that the white to black wealth ratio is 20 to 1. What are some current dynamics or trends that we are seeing in race, wealth, and debt in this supposedly "post-recession" era?

Dalton Conley: Over time, the racial wealth gap has hovered around 10 to 1, meaning that the median African American family has 10% of the wealth, or the net worth, of the median white family. "Net worth" is the value in the marketplace of all your belongings and assets that you can sell. If you sell everything you own and pay off all your debts, the amount of money left over is your net worth, and that's what we mean by wealth.

With legacies of slavery and the civil rights era, African Americans are kind of latecomers to the wealth accumulation game for a variety of historical and institutional reasons associated with the history of race and discrimination in the United States. As blacks typically are overrepresented among the unemployed and low-wealth households, the more that wealth becomes unequally distributed in general across society, the more unequal the racial wealth gap.

The black-white wealth gap has ebbed and flowed over the course of the century, peaking at about 40% in 1929 before the financial crash that led to the Great Depression and in 2007, with a period in the middle of the century that was more equal. While the security markets have bounced back since the financial crisis of 2008, housing markets have not rebounded as much, particularly in low-income areas. If anything, the wealth gap has been accentuated by the Great Recession.

Rachel Dwyer: The current dynamics in the racial wealth gap are a mix of entrenched inequalities with deeply concerning new developments. The racial wealth gap has long been driven by housing inequality undergirded by continued high levels of residential segregation. New political economic dynamics have changed the nature of black-white housing inequality, however. Whereas blocked access to mortgages was once the principal obstacle to black homeownership, loosened financial regulation means that inequalities in mortgage terms and conditions like interest rates, payment terms, and loan servicing increasingly drive housing inequality. Douglas Massey has described these changes as the "moving target" in housing discrimination.

Karyn Lacy: The most important trend impacting the black-white wealth gap in the current period is the fall-out from the foreclosure crisis, which began in 2006. Two and a half million people lost their homes between 2007 and 2009. Because a home is the most valuable (often only) asset that the average American owns, it is the primary means of accumulating wealth. Rates of homeownership are significantly higher among whites than blacks, in part because financing a dream home has involved different processes for white home seekers than for blacks. The financing options of both groups have been shaped historically by the discriminatory practices of Realtors, lenders, and the federal government—groups that have helped to construct and perpetuate a dual housing market, providing a clear path to homeownership for whites while obstructing the homeownership aspirations of upwardly mobile blacks.

A different problem emerged in the mid-1990s. A new class of lenders, motivated by the potential for quick profits, was *eager* to grant mortgages to blacks. The problem is that the terms of these *subprime* loans triggered a new form of inequitable lending characterized by deceptive loan terms. There are many different types of subprime loans, but the most common type is the adjustable-rate mortgage (ARM), loans that start off at a low interest rate and corresponding monthly payment, but are designed to rise sharply at an established future date. In 2006, 55% of black borrowers held subprime loans, and when these loans reset at higher interest rates, the outrageous terms tipped many borrowers toward default.

Dwyer: Discussions of the racial wealth gap must start with housing, but they should not end there. Racial dynamics related to savings for retirement and indebtedness from student loans and credit cards have only just begun to be understood. The fraying of the social safety net combined with increasing uncertainty in the American economy has resulted in what Jacob Hacker has called the "great risk shift," making racial wealth inequalities potentially even more consequential for life chances than they have been in the past. Broad shifts like the decline of pensions and rising expectations that individuals will prepare for their own retirement hit black Americans particularly hard because of the preexisting wealth disadvantage.

Declining public support for education means those seeking social mobility must rely more on student loans. Access to consumer debt has undergone the same kind of diversification and complexity as mortgages, creating new forms of racial inequality in debt holding, perhaps most notably in the area of short-term and payday loans.

In your opinion, what are the most pressing current issues around race, wealth, and debt? Are there policy initiatives that are, or should be, addressing these issues?

Dwyer: One key issue is ensuring equal access to good credit for all racial groups. The huge problems with indebtedness that surfaced during the financial crisis should not lead us to conclude that all debt is bad. We need to strengthen financial regulation to require transparency and consumer protections to maintain credit availability, but reduce individual and systemic risk. This is needed for all forms of debt, including mortgages, consumer credit, and student loans. Better regulation is particularly needed for the short-term and payday loans that ravage poor minority communities and families. If we wish to benefit as a society from the positive results of wide access to credit, then we also need to have fair and transparent access to bankruptcy provisions (including for student loans) for the cases when those debts go sour. Clearly, better enforcement of antidiscrimination laws is also required to provide equal access to high-quality credit.

Lacy: Even in the postrecession era, when federal policy has scaled back subprime lending, we are still observing the long-term effects of predatory lending on homeownership and wealth accumulation. A growing problem is that predatory lenders have come up with novel ways to circumvent new legislation designed to protect unsuspecting homeowners. For example, once a loan is sold on the secondary market, the new lender may not change the terms of the loan, but new lenders avoid this constraint by simply tacking on a long list of exorbitant fees, from late fees to so-called processing fees assessed against borrowers who pay by check or money order rather than online. These practices impose a significant financial burden on borrowers who are barely managing to make their scheduled payments and borrowers who do not have checking accounts or a personal computer.

Conley: If we define net worth as assets minus debts, for some people that ends up being a negative. Quite a lot of people nowadays are underwater on their mortgages, meaning that the amount they owe exceeds the equity in the home because the value has crashed. So, another way to think about the relationship between race and wealth is to ask what is the proportion that is overall underwater or in the red. Of the people with negative net worth, we see a huge racial disparity there, too. Blacks are way overrepresented in the group that is in the red, that has negative net worth. So, debt, of course, is as important as savings and asset accumulation—it's just the other side of the coin.

The political reality is that it's going to take a million little issues, a million little policies to try to nudge things in the right direction, and that's probably the best we can hope for. Right now we have a lot of policies that help the rich get richer; we don't have a lot that help the poor get a leg up. We could address this through things like capping the amount of home mortgage deduction that people can take and promoting wealth production among those who are at the bottom end of the distribution. Even if we did all those things, I'm not sure it would fix the problem entirely.

Dwyer: Rebuilding the social safety net is particularly important for racial-minority populations who have less individual and family wealth than the average white family to fall back on as a personal safety net. If we had a better safety net, then fewer Americans would need to turn to usurious and predatory lending. A broad approach that addressed the rising economic precarity of many Americans from all racial and ethnic groups could build coalitions across racial dividing lines and develop the social solidarity that is needed to support ambitious social insurance initiatives. Scholars frequently highlight racial antagonisms as one key factor in explaining why social welfare in the U.S. has been so anemic compared to other developed countries. Paradoxically, rising inequality and precarity in American life could bring a greater awareness that economic vulnerability is an issue for all racial groups, and greater support for policies that lower the costs of losing out for all.

In what ways do specific types of debt (such as, say, credit card debt in contrast to a mortgage) privilege different racial and socioeconomic groups while disadvantaging others?

Conley: Debt itself is not necessarily an evil thing, especially if it allows us to make an investment we wouldn't otherwise be able to make. If you borrow money for college, at least in theory, we like to think that educational debt is worth it because you're going to get a better job afterwards. You're investing in human capital and you're going to be able to pay that back easily with the additional wages that you'll get from going to college.

However, not all debt is treated equally. For example, the interest you pay on a home mortgage, because of U.S. policy to promote homeownership, is tax deductible, but that tax deduction is not even capped. If you take out a 2 or 3 million dollar mortgage, you are able to deduct the interest from your taxes at the same rate for each individual dollar of interest you pay as someone who has a $20,000 mortgage on a home. I agree that we need policy to be encouraging, but I don't think that we need to incentivize luxury homeownership.

Compared to mortgages, educational loans operate very differently. For instance, if you file for bankruptcy, student loan debt is not forgiven. Because of pressure and lobbying from the loan companies, student debt follows you to the grave no matter what.

Dwyer: The issue is what kinds of credit do different groups have access to and thereby what kinds of risks do they face? All credit carries risk. Racial and socioeconomic groups are differentiated in access to different types of credit with different levels of risk. Sometimes this differentiated access operates through discrimination and prejudice. Sometimes this differentiated access occurs as a result of inequalities in resources (which may, of course, be caused or worsened by discrimination as well). For example, it is usually better to hold debt on a credit card than in a payday loan. But some groups do not qualify for a credit card and therefore are restricted in the types of loans they can get. This means that more white and affluent people can benefit from lower-cost and better-termed credit than many minority and poor people. This is an instance of David Caplovitz's classic insight that "the poor pay more."

Lacy: One of the most pressing concerns is the misrepresentation of the causes and scope of the foreclosure crisis in the public sphere. Speaking from the floor of the House, Representative Bachmann argued that unwise decisions on the part of black borrowers *caused* the housing crisis. The media play a role too, as one headline after another asks whether the foreclosure crisis has decimated the black middle class. The focus on black borrowers to the exclusion of other troubled borrowers has made blacks the public face of the foreclosure crisis. But studies of the crisis reveal that high-income Hispanic and Asian homeowners foreclose at higher rates than any other group. These borrowers are concentrated in "boom markets," states where the steep housing prices exceeded the national average prior to the economic crisis and plummeted during the crisis, making these high-income, minority borrowers vulnerable to foreclosure.

How does inequality in wealth and debt influence other forms of inequality?

Lacy: Wealth inequality depresses a family's opportunities to provide the good life for their children. Persistent residential segregation contributes to this problem. Property values rise less rapidly in predominately black neighborhoods than they do in majority white neighborhoods, depriving many black homeowners of the kind of equity accumulation that could be parlayed into financing a child's college education or helping an adult child to start a business or purchase a home of their own.

Dwyer: There are a great many ways that wealth inequalities impinge on life chances, because wealth levels affect whether a family can invest in education or a home; how a person or family survives shocks like a job loss, divorce, or medical crisis; and the amount and type of intergenerational transfers. There are also important interactions between debt holding and asset accrual that have implications for wealth inequality itself. Some take on debt to accelerate asset accrual (this is the hope for many homeowners). For others, debt holding is a net drain that weakens wealth accrual or even draws down savings. Some forms of wealth provide new types of credit access, like home equity loans and some forms of retirement savings, but taking out that credit can sometimes end up destroying the collateral asset. The financialization of the U.S. economy and the increasing diversity of financial instruments available to average Americans make these issues of financial well-being increasingly important for life chances and particularly important for racial minorities struggling to achieve wealth mobility.

Conley: My research examines the effects of this wealth disparity. I look at what predicts how far kids get economically in life, whether they get a four-year college degree, work in a professional occupation, and how much income and wealth they end up earning and accumulating in their lifetimes. I find that of all the measured factors of their parents, of the family they grew up in, only two matter: number one is their parents' education level and number two is their parents' wealth level. Wealth inequality, then, is driving racial inequality and class inequality in a number of other dimensions. I don't mean to say that race doesn't matter because race itself is almost the best predictor of wealth levels, but that wealth gap itself then becomes the perpetuator of racial inequality in the next generation. Essentially, it's this kind of vicious circle: Race predicts wealth but then wealth predicts—along with education—everything else. Each generation keeps reproducing itself.

PARTICIPANT PROFILES

Dalton Conley is in the sociology department at New York University. A prolific writer, his book *Being Black, Living in the Red* (UC Press, 2009) examines the effects of economic inequality on African Americans.

Rachel Dwyer is a professor in the sociology department at the Ohio State University. Her research explores economic inequality, particularly young people and debt.

Karyn Lacy is in the sociology department at the University of Michigan. Her research focuses on the intersections of race and class, particularly in the experiences of black middle-class suburbanites in the United States.

TSP tie-in

objective debt, subjective inequalities

Money is far from neutral: it's personal. A powerful new set of studies in *Sociological Quarterly* and *Sociological Forum* shows how debt is fraught with emotion, subjectivity, and the lived experiences of individuals striving to survive in turbulent economic times. Sociologists are beginning to capture the personal side of the financial crisis, particularly the relationship between creditor and debtor.

Sociologists Randy Hodson, Rachel Dwyer, and Lisa Neilson show that credit functions as a resource for some and a liability for many others. They describe debt as infused with a "special social and moral meaning" that resides in the consciences of its holders. The "democratization of credit" has introduced new forms of debt to borrowers from all socio-economic strata. Among those with unsecured debt (i.e., not car loans, housing and property debt, or student loan debt), however, they find middle-class Americans experienced the greatest levels of anxiety and depression related to their finances—both before *and* after the recession. To ease such financial distress, Hodson, Dwyer, and Neilson argue that we need *better* credit, rather than *more* credit.

Still, most of us blame ourselves for our credit problems, rather than the conditions of our borrowing. Sociologist Karen McCormack conducted 36 interviews with participants in two foreclosure-prevention workshops in Boston and Lawrence, Massachusetts, to understand how "at-risk" borrowers attribute responsibility for the foreclosure crisis. She found that most borrowers perceived the loss of a home as an individual failing, in spite of the broader trends of foreclosure. Many also tried to increase their self-worth by denigrating others. That is, they rejected the notion that their *own* foreclosure was the result of some personal shortcoming, but labeled other borrowers in similar circumstances "irresponsible." The struggle these homeowners had in shifting responsibility for their situation to broader structural understandings of the global financial crisis reflects our moralized relationship with credit and creditors.

This moral relationship is also shaped by intervening organizations, such as debt-settlement agencies. Sociologists Francesca Polletta and Zaibu Tufail conducted field observations at two debt-settlement agencies and interviews with 17 agents to learn why clients are willing to settle certain forms of debt over others. They found that debtors distinguished between credit card debt and medical debt, concluding that decisions about repayment were based on perceptions of the moral character of the creditor. Debtors saw less integrity in the bureaucratic ethos of credit card companies, relative to the greater trust they placed in the moral worth of medical providers. Debtors were therefore more willing to settle (rather than fully repay) credit card claims. Even when the debts were equal (in dollars), medical debt represented a moral obligation based on personal interactions with someone who played a role in healing. In contrast, impersonal ties with credit card companies mean their demands for repayment often fail to elicit guilt and a sense of obligation. In other words, when settling debt, we are not only making good with creditors but with our consciences too.

The new sociology of debt shows how the process of discrediting the debtor as stigmatized "burdens" or irresponsible people is linked to existing class hierarchies and unequal power relations. In many cases, the interpersonal costs of debt are likely greater than its monetary value. Shifting attention to the more subjective side of debt also shifts our perceptions of those mired in it. Whether they sink or swim depends as much on their social and cultural capital as it does on their economic capital. Debt is not an equal opportunity construct but is socially structured in moralized terms and under highly unequal conditions.

—RAHSAAN MAHADEO

cultural contexts

students squeezed by an hourglass economy

ROBERT CROSNOE

A few years ago, I visited classrooms filled with poor and working-class students in a diverse high school in Texas; I was launching a long-term study on teenage social life that formed the basis for my book *Fitting In, Standing Out*. Because I was the first professor many students had ever met, they grilled me about what it took to go to college, and I responded by asking them many questions about their future plans. In addition to the fact that, apparently, all teenagers now want to be forensic investigators, one thing that struck me was just how uniform their college expectations were. Every kid, regardless of background, wanted to go to college. Few had a concrete idea of how to make that happen.

This mixture of hope, ambition, and, for lack of a better word, *cluelessness* that I saw crystallized for me how higher education can simultaneously reduce and fuel inequality in the United States. The truth is that college *has* become more important than ever, but getting there is often a murky process that puts a premium on many factors beyond academic merit. In this process, youth from low socioeconomic status (SES) families are at a distinct disadvantage. Unlike their better-off peers, they cannot count on their parents and grandparents setting up college funds or using their connections to get them into the best schools and programs.

Critically discussing today's push toward college is important. Much like the "Just Say No" antidrug campaign of the 1980s was criticized for being simplistic and unrealistic, "Just Go to College" is too facile a response to many of the problems of inequality the United States faces as it emerges from the depths of the Great Recession. We need to go beyond bromides to understand the challenges involved in getting into, going to, graduating from, and paying for college, and we need plans to address each step. Because each of these challenges reflects socioeconomic disadvantages passed down across generations, the success of efforts to support the children in poor and working-class families might very well rest on what we can do to help their parents.

college matters

A college degree meant more for me in the long run than it did for my parents, and it will likely mean much more for my children than for me. Although the recent onslaught of news stories about college graduates going straight to the unemployment line creates the perception that this upsurge in the value of a college degree has taken a hit during the Great Recession, that perception is false. A variety of historical trends explains why.

Historically, the U.S. economy was based in manufacturing. As a result, the labor market was shaped like a pyramid, with a small supply of high-value, high-demand occupations requiring special training at the top. In the middle came a large supply of stable, nonprofessional jobs with benefits that required only a high school diploma. These jobs allowed Americans to gain a secure economic foothold and sponsor the social mobility of the next generation. In the classic example, poor parents who work in a menial job (at the wide base of the pyramid) would send their children into the public K–12 system. Those children would then use their high school education to land jobs on an auto assembly line (in the middle of the pyramid), thereby providing the resources for their own children to go to college, start a business, and/or become professionals. If all went well, the third generation could top the pyramid.

Since the late 1960s, however, the economy has shifted into an information/service phase—Apple has replaced GM, as it were. New kinds of skills are sought and rewarded. The resulting hourglass-shaped labor market has a broad stratum of well-paying, high-skilled jobs at the top and an even broader stratum of insecure, low-skilled jobs at the bottom, with very little in between. Higher education has become the most effective way to push through the bottleneck, dramatically increasing the payoff of making the leap from high school into college. An illustration of these rising returns is the earnings premium, or the increased percentage of earnings that comes with a college degree. According to the College Board, the premium was between 20 and 30% when I was born in the early 1970s but had skyrocketed to well over 65% by the time my children were born in the 2000s.

Thinking of returns solely in terms of money, however, would be a mistake. Going to college brings many other advantages in life—from the durability of marriage to good mental health to life expectancy.

Importantly, sociologists Jennie Brand and Yu Xie have shown that many of the returns on higher education are greater for youth who are least likely to go to college, such as those from socioeconomically disadvantaged backgrounds. This finding makes perfect sense. Yet, as documented by many economists, the increase in American youth attending and graduating from college over the last several decades has come primarily at the upper tails of the socioeconomic distribution. In other words, poor and working-class youth have more to gain from going to college but are less likely to do so.

Efforts to interrupt the intergenerational cycle of socio-economic inequality, therefore, must break down the barriers that keep youth from lower-SES backgrounds from realizing the opportunities for social mobility that college represents. These efforts can be informed by understanding how the path to college plays out over long periods of time and is deeply connected to the personal histories and current circumstances of parents.

recognizing the obstacles

We've known since the famous Coleman Report—a 1966 study funded by Congress—that schools serving lower-SES populations have less academic rigor, a worse resource base, and poor instructional quality relative to those serving more socio-economically advantaged communities. After 13 years of often drastically unequal schooling, students from poor and working-class backgrounds are less prepared to ace the high-stakes tests that weigh so heavily in college admissions, let alone the challenges of college coursework if admitted. What may seem to some like a meritocratic competition (that is, colleges admitting high school seniors based on their academic records) is merely the tail end of a long journey of inequality.

One caveat to this pattern is the "frog pond effect": Is it better to be a big frog in a small pond or a small frog in a big pond? When test scores and grades are held constant, a student attending an underprivileged high school is somewhat *more* likely than a student attending a more competitive high school to be admitted to the college of his or her choice. What needs to be stressed, though, is years of school inequality would mean the former student would be less likely to *get* to that equivalent academic position than the latter. This dualism of frog pond effects—an *apparent* exception to and *actual* example of inequality—has been illustrated for me by the rancor over a policy here in Texas. It grants automatic admission to state flagships for top-ranked graduates of Texas public high schools, regardless of which school. An attempt to expand access to college to students from the most disadvantaged communities in the state, the "Top 10 Percent Plan," has been accused of favoring highly ranked students at struggling schools over "better" students ranked lower in their classes at more competitive schools.

Another caveat is that the focus on the path to college begins *before* K–12 schooling. Young children from lower-SES families have less cognitive stimulation and structured learning in and out of the home and are less likely to attend preschool than better-off kids. They enter school with underdeveloped academic skills, and, although this disparity might reflect learning opportunities more than learning abilities, it sets children on divergent academic trajectories by affecting teacher expectations and curricular positions. As sociologists of education Doris Entwisle, Karl Alexander, and colleagues have illustrated over the years, the cumulative nature of the K–12 system means that even small differences in school readiness can compound into large end-of-school differences. Growing awareness has led to calls for expanding preschool access—calls bolstered by econometric evidence that early interventions bring greater long-term returns on investment than those targeting later stages of schooling.

As important as they are, differences in school quality cannot completely explain socioeconomic disparities in college attendance. More interpersonal processes are also at work. Sociologists like Stephen L. Morgan and Annette Lareau have illuminated the subtle ways that students from lower-SES families are at a competitive disadvantage because they know less about what factors go into college admissions and how they are weighed. Unlike their higher-SES peers, their parents cannot finance supplemental supports (e.g., tutors and admissions consultants) to demystify the admissions process, nor can they draw on knowledge from their own personal histories and social connections about courses, activities, and other résumé entries that different colleges might value.

I once interviewed two motivated girls about their college plans. The one from a working-class background said that her mother counseled her to better her chances of getting into college by boosting her overall GPA and appearing well rounded, even if that meant dropping out of advanced math and science classes and replacing them with courses like sign language. The other, a daughter of college graduates, opined that good grades and activities would not mean much without a rigorous course load; her parents had insisted that taking calculus now would mean that she could place out of it once she got to college. Despite similar abilities, the former student was clearly less well positioned to get into and stay in the college of her choice than the latter. Such uninformed versus informed decision making is a window into how SES is transferred from parent to child. The sociology literature abounds with other examples, such as pushy high-SES parents getting their children into curricula above their abilities, the weight of "legacies" in admissions, and the proactive efforts to serve students with high-SES parents.

Of course, money does matter, and not just through its power to boost school quality and provide supplemental support. Attending college can bring huge financial costs, and students from poor and working-class families are often unable to afford the sticker price, not to mention all the non-tuition expenses, including books, room and board, and more frequent incidental costs like fast-food and coffee purchases. Moreover, youth from such families may not have a good sense of what all those costs are, and they tend to have less of a handle on financial aid and the other support that may be available to them, despite being the primary intended recipients.

a strategy for side-by-side scholars

Many risks that I have covered here are rooted in how much money parents have, and parents' finances are intricately related to their own educational attainment. Other risks are rooted in differences in the nonmonetary advantages that some parents have. These, too, are tied to their educational histories. Given this centrality of parent education to the risk equation, one method of promoting socioeconomic equity in college attendance in the United States might be to raise the educational attainment of lower-SES *parents*.

Yes, this idea can be quickly dismissed as both circular and too late in the game. After all, as teenagers approach the transition into college, their parents' educational careers would seem to be long past done. Yet, research shows that many Americans—especially disadvantaged Americans—accrue education discontinuously, often after becoming parents. Furthermore, evidence is accumulating that parents who return to higher education while their children are still in grade school increase their active management of their children's education in ways that promote academic progress. In addition to the financial boost that education brings, such parents may learn more about how education works, feel more efficacious dealing with school personnel, be better information seekers and consumers, and have higher expectations for their kids (after all, if mom is studying in the evening, why wouldn't she expect her kids to do the same?). Again, these effects are likely to be strongest for the most disadvantaged Americans. This U.S. pattern echoes the two-generation tradition in international aid and development of investing in the education of parents to promote the long-term educational interests of children.

Taking a two-generation approach to socioeconomic disparities in college attendance is a long-term strategy. By supporting the school enrollment of socioeconomically disadvantaged parents of young children today, both government and nonprofit programs may increase the flow of those children into the college pipeline tomorrow. To date, evidence that such programs (for instance, the recently defunct federal program Even Start) work is mixed, but low investment in these programs and their short duration are possible reasons for underperformance. In thinking big about the problem, a long-term strategy is worth a closer look; it aligns well with what we know to be some of the greatest risks facing children from low-SES families on the path to college.

Two-generation investment is a specific idea that is part of a larger need to inject fresh thinking into research and policy intervention. If higher education matters so much in the United States, then more must be done to even out socioeconomic disparities in college attendance—by addressing the financial terms of the equation, yes, but also by targeting the many noneconomic mechanisms that keep youth with lower-SES parents from realizing college dreams.

At the same time, we need to start a bit of a tricky conversation: How can we make higher education matter *less*? In other words, we've got to identify viable ways for youth to develop skills and find security in the labor market without going to college. As recent reports about debt loads and dropouts in the burgeoning online college market suggest, we still have more to do to answer this question. Whether children coming of age in the Great Recession are going to end up a lost generation, squeezed by an hourglass economy, depends on what we do now.

RECOMMENDED READING

Paul Attewell, David E. Lavin, Thurston Domina, and Tania Levey. 2007. *Passing the Torch: Does Higher Education for the Disadvantaged Pay Off Across the Generations?* New York: Russell

Sage Foundation. A fascinating study of the educational performance of parents and their children over three decades that demonstrates how promoting socioeconomically disadvantaged youths' access to higher education can pay off in future generations.

Claudia Goldin and Lawrence F. Katz. 2008. *The Race between Education and Technology.* Cambridge, MA: Harvard University Press. An explanation of long-term trends in the U.S. (and global) economy that have dramatically increased the value of going to college.

Eric Grodsky and Erika Jackson. 2010. "Social Stratification in Higher Education." *Teachers College Record* 111:2347–2384. A thorough and thoughtful review on inequality and education, emphasizing institutions as well as students.

Thomas J. Kane. 1999. *The Price of Admission: Rethinking How Americans Pay for College.* Washington, DC: Brookings Institution Press. A discussion of why the costs of higher education have risen, the challenges this poses to socioeconomically disadvantaged youth, and the policies and programs that have potential to help.

debt and darkness in detroit

DAVID SCHALLIOL

6

The owner of a southwest Detroit convenience store knew he'd had enough: A customer had walked out into the night and was promptly robbed on the store's front step.

The owner was frustrated by vacant buildings and an overstretched police force, but the darkness was most infuriating. The closest streetlight had been out for four years. The next closest had just gone out. Now thieves weren't so much lurking in the shadows as simply standing, waiting for victims to literally walk into them.

Social life changes dramatically when cities can't provide the taken-for-granted basics of urban living—just a streetlamp can make all the difference. With no anticipated help from the city, the shop owner adjusted the one thing he could control: He ringed his building with new lights and switched out old bulbs for brighter, more energy-efficient models.

Light spilled out from his store to the surrounding streets, illuminating the sidewalks, his gravel parking area, and the nearby vacant lots.

Nearly three years later, his lights are still the only ones illuminating his section of the street, but most nearby businesses have followed the shop owner's lead and installed their own floodlights. The patchwork effort may not make up for the lack of streetlights, but this private provision of a public good is a start.

In some ways, this dismal situation is no surprise. Detroit has become the symbolic bellwether for the national economy, and its problems have been catalogued by nearly every major newspaper, magazine, and television program. From photography books labeled "ruin porn" to feature films scanning the veneer of the city, a growing body of material tries to make sense of the rise and fall of the Motor City. The coverage may actually be disproportionate. While Detroit's financial problems *are* monumental, the coverage obscures what those in many "postindustrial" cities know: Detroit's problems are shared by dozens of municipalities across the country and many more around the world.

going bankrupt

Wracked by the common maladies of white flight, deindustrialization, and poverty, Detroit hasn't received much good news in the last several decades. The formal culmination of these problems came when Michigan's governor appointed attorney Kevyn Orr Detroit's "emergency manager" in March 2013. While many residents protested the decision as stripping power from the elected city council and Mayor Dave Bing, the governor touted Orr's experience working with troubled institutions, including Detroit-connected companies like Chrysler. Among the new manager's authorities would be the ability to recommend the initiation of bankruptcy proceedings, which he did swiftly.

Jaye Dee's Mart stands on the edge of several dark blocks.
© David Schalliol

Orr's July 2013 Proposal for Creditors outlines many of Detroit's problems: Property tax revenues declined nearly 20% and income taxes 15% over the last five years. The utility users' excise tax receipts were down 28% over the previous decade. Even the state's contribution to the city, made through a revenue-sharing agreement, was down more than 30% since 2008. The one bright spot in the revenue picture was that wagering taxes were holding, but the emergency manager cautioned they, too, would decline once casinos opened in nearby Toledo in 2015.

The fact is, Detroit has accumulated more than $18 billion in debt and unfunded liabilities from regular deficit spending, pension expansion, and debt-restructuring deals that only exacerbate the problem. The city is expected to have a "negative cash flow" of nearly $200 million in the next fiscal year, and, if something isn't done about the debt, the majority of the city's general fund may be swallowed by debt service payments within the next few years.

The results have been catastrophic for citizens: Detroit's violent crime rate is the highest of any major U.S. city, emergency services response times are abysmal, and the city is plagued by 78,000 derelict buildings and another 66,000 derelict lots it doesn't have the money to clean up or maintain. There have been more than 110,000 fires in the last 10 years; approximately 60% were in unoccupied structures. In a tragic irony, even the internationally renowned Heidelberg Project, which reuses derelict houses as art installations, has been the victim of arson in the past year. As of early December 2013, five of the building installations have been burned, despite efforts by the police, the Bureau of Alcohol, Tobacco, Firearms and Explosives, private security, and the fire department. The Heidelberg Project just completed a fund-raising initiative to support the installation of permanent security cameras, guards, and solar-powered lights.

streetlights and fear

While policing, abandonment, and public service disruptions have been covered in the media, the story of darkness is relatively new. The emergency manager's report concluded that approximately 40% of the 88,000 streetlights in Detroit are "not functioning due, in large part, to disrepair and neglect." The rate is the worst in the nation.

An aging system and burned-out bulbs cause some of the streetlight outages, but a variety of other factors are in play. Windstorms have been particularly problematic for the system, which often still relies on aboveground lines. Trees haven't been trimmed, so gusts of wind regularly break branches and cause localized power outages. Illegal scrap metal collectors run rampant, stripping valuable wiring from abandoned buildings and utilities. One recent high-profile case even involved the state-controlled lights flanking Interstate 94. Thieves posing as utility workers parked their trucks near the newly updated lighting system and stole thousands of dollars of copper wiring in the middle of the day. Elsewhere, others simply break the streetlights for fun or to remain in the dark.

While the state will have to deal with its own losses, the city's declining revenues mean that the Department of Public Lighting is astonishingly underfunded, unable to address even basic complaints. Reporter and media personality Charlie LeDuff famously visited the department's facilities, describing one substation as "so old, it reminds one of Dr. Frankenstein's laboratory" and the main office as looking "like a neutron bomb went off in 1959." He was incredulous to learn that fewer than 10 employees are responsible for maintaining Detroit's lights.

With so few service personnel, a common refrain from the public is that the city doesn't respond. The city's data support their concerns: There was a backlog of nearly 3,300 complaints regarding streetlight outages in April 2013. One southwest Detroit party store owner lamented, "There's a system from the city to put in a request, but I hate dealing with anybody down there. They don't do nothin'." Lengthy delays feel like inaction, whether generated by resource scarcity, ambivalence, negligence, or incompetence. As a result, many residents look to their neighbors or other informal channels to address the problem.

These concerns might simply generate local community action and a vote of no confidence in city government if it weren't for another factor: the relationship between fear of crime and the darkness.

Even when crime is at its worst, it is not omnipresent—but residents know darkness comes every night. A middle-aged north side resident lamented, "I know a lot of people who don't come out once it gets dark because there aren't enough lights outside. They try to get stuff done during the day. But that's also related to all of the crime in the city. And the dark just makes it worse." Seasonal differences and the shift to standard time produce greater problems: "We have more worries about light in the wintertime than in the summer, 'cause in the summer it's light out until 9, 9:30, but in the winter months it gets dark at 4:30 and is pitch black at 5. People start to worry."

The darkness is particularly hard on those who don't have cars or can't afford the gas to drive. A store owner along an active stretch of Livernois Avenue relayed, "Their problem is getting to the store. . . . They're worried people could stalk them. If they're coming from a subdivision, there are absolutely no lights. Eventually they get to the main streets, there are a little more lights, but not enough." A resident who works in the Woodbridge neighborhood near Wayne State University agreed: "I like it lit up at nighttime. I can see. I don't like nobody coming up behind me, nobody I can't see.... You can't see nothing in the dark."

For many Detroit residents, particularly dark places have become associated with criminal activity. Although detailed study of the night is surprisingly underdeveloped, a general fear of the night is assumed or supported in most urban research and even built into the General Social Survey. Criminologists Brandon Welsh and David Farrington demonstrate convincingly that street lighting does reduce crime—not just by deterring criminals at night but by increasing community pride and informal control during the day. But there is reason to believe the experience of Detroit (and cities in its position) may be even more pronounced. In Detroit, not only does a general sense of anxiety hover over the night, but the assumption that emergency services will arrive "too late, if ever" undermines even the weakest elements of the social contract. The crux of the situation may be how individuals react to the urban night without confidence in local government.

It is established that fear of crime transforms communities, but *how* they are transformed is based on community characteristics. Since economist Albert Hirschman's *Exit,*

Voice, and Loyalty, urban scholars have looked at the processes that influence whether residents will leave a neighborhood or remain when confronted with a problem. If they remain, will they attempt to influence the situation? Or will they simply be neglectful, identifying a problem but doing nothing? Characteristics that influence community members' responses are varied. Some research locates the decision to stay and fight around semistructural factors like access to financial and organizational resources. Here, the capacity to mobilize a broad range of institutional resources is instrumental to addressing community problems. Other research links the decision to an individual's perception of the social situation. Residents are more willing to engage if they believe neighbors might share an interest in responding to the problem or if they think the neighborhood is improving.

Clearly, Detroit's population decline (the city has lost more than 1.1 million residents since its peak in 1950) demonstrates that the dominant decision has been to leave. But will those who choose to remain fight to improve Detroit or just let the problems fester? What influences their decision? Store- and homeowners who install lights express elements of a "voice," although this is a relatively low-cost action that may only reveal a limited engagement with their community.

We can learn more by looking to the select sections of the city that are experiencing the first population growth in years. While most of the city's neighborhoods suffer from the darkness, the places experiencing growth tend to be those relatively protected from it.

The relatively affluent downtown has become the subject of countless news stories. Its lauded resurgence has been orchestrated by business executives like Quicken Loans' Dan Gilbert, who has urged employees to move downtown and employed private security forces to circle downtown streets. Executives' efforts have meant that lights have been upgraded, stabilized, and even augmented in the busiest areas. A some-what more organic pattern is occurring in other growing areas like the near-southwest Corktown neighborhood and its active Michigan Avenue stretch, as well as in Midtown, a neighborhood associated with cultural institutions like the now-threatened Detroit Institute of Arts. A southwest business district raised more than $6 million for streetlight improvements along a major thoroughfare. As even those far from downtown know, "The main reason we put in the lights was two things: one, is for safety. . . . Two, they attract attention. When everything else is dark, it calls attention to the store."

The coupling of individual and group actions throughout the city, alongside the grand public-private redevelopment of downtown, is a stopgap measure. Even before the bankruptcy groundwork was devised, state and local officials were attempting to address the streetlight problem. The Public Lighting Authority of Detroit was created by the state legislature and city council to "develop and implement a plan to improve public lighting in the city of Detroit." Currently in a pilot stage, the initiative plans to rebuild the *entire* lighting system over the course of three years, while strategically eliminating approximately half of the city's current streetlights. Though the total number of active streetlights will remain near current levels, the authority promises its efforts will efficiently and reliably produce more light in the "right" places, including every intersection. In so doing, it is setting the stage for anticipated improvement in other public service provisions that can move forward with the city's bankruptcy.

So, where is this new entity getting its funding? The Public Lighting Authority of Detroit will take on $210 million in new debt.

Detroit's bankruptcy proceedings, lighting programs, and other initiatives provide unique opportunities to understand how communities change in response to wholesale structural and environmental changes. They also provide an opportunity to take lessons beyond the city to ensure they are applied in neighborhoods of all conditions.

Mixed lighting is cast by different sources in midtown. © *David Schalliol*

A man stands next to his bike outside a well-lit store. © *David Schalliol*

A closed but still illuminated liquor store. © *David Schalliol*

El Durango Bar lights up its block. © *David Schalliol*

A southwest side party store illuminates its area. © *David Schalliol*

A laundromat and broken streetlight at sunset in the Mexican-town neighborhood. © *David Schalliol*

A liquor store's sign and lights cut through smoke on Fort Street.
© David Schalliol

A downtown store decorated with holiday lights. © David Schalliol

A couple walks by a southwest side house. © *David Schalliol*

A house casts light into the adjacent empty lots. © *David Schalliol*

RECOMMENDED READING

Robert J. Sampson. 2012. *Great American City: Chicago and the Enduring Neighborhood Effect* (Revised edition). Chicago: University of Chicago Press. A current evaluation of the relationship between neighborhoods and social organization.

Thomas J. Sugrue. 2005. *The Origins of the Urban Crisis: Race and Inequality in Postwar Detroit* (Revised edition). Princeton, NJ: Princeton University Press. A formative history of the causes and consequences of Detroit's dramatic postwar decline.

Richard P. Taub, D. Garth Taylor, and Jan D. Dunham. 1984. *Paths of Neighborhood Change: Race and Crime in Urban America*. Chicago: University of Chicago Press. An early contemporary assessment of the factors that influence a neighborhood's rise or fall.

Brandon C. Welsh and David P. Farrington. 2008. *Effects of Improved Street Lighting on Crime*. The Campbell Collaboration: Campbell Systematic Reviews. Evidence about why and how street lighting reduces crime.

andrew ross on the anti-debt movement

ERIN HOEKSTRA

B
y now, it's clear that in the United States and around the world, debt has come to shape people's lives. Some use debt to get ahead, others buy debt to make a profit, and still others find their choices constrained by the weight of the debt they are dragging around. Andrew Ross, author of *Creditocracy and the Case for Debt Refusal* (OR Books, 2014), is convinced that finances have become modern shackles and that only an effective, equality-based social movement can loosen those bonds. The full audio of Ross's Office Hours interview is available at thesocietypages.org/inequality.

Erin Hoekstra: What do you mean by "creditocracy"?

Andrew Ross: A creditocracy is a society in which the majority of people are so deeply in debt that it can never be repaid. Creditocracy emerges when the cost of access to social goods is privately held individual debt. These social goods are not just things that improve quality of life, but basic requirements of life, including housing, education, health care, and even putting food on the table, which for many people requires going into debt. In this kind of society, our society, the creditor's goal is to wrap debt around every single possible asset or income stream, ensuring a flow of interest. In a particularly advanced stage of a creditocracy, debtors have to seek out fresh sources of credit simply to service their existing debt. One of the bumper stickers I cite summarizes that condition: "I use MasterCard to pay Visa." For the working poor, this has long been a familiar arrangement, but in recent decades, the position of permanent indebtedness has moved up into the higher reaches of social strata and now affects at least one, maybe two, generations of the college-educated middle class. That is the more advanced phase of creditocracy.

Hoekstra: You argue that our current system of debt and credit is holding Americans in a sort of "debt bondage." How does it impact people's lives on a daily basis?

Ross: *Debt bondage* is a very strong term, an inflammatory term for some, but it's part of the revival of historical systems of and ways of talking about debt, including classic forms of debt bondage under feudalism, slavery, indenture, and all its successor institutions like sharecropping and loan sharking. The legacy of all those forms of debt bondage is very much alive and well on the subprime landscape of fringe finance. Payday loan facilities, check-cashing facilities, all the poverty banks that operate on "loan alley" are increasingly making their way onto Main Street because they're moving upscale. Debt bondage, something that has affected people on a daily basis in low-income communities, is moving up into the middle class. We're also seeing a revival of talk about indenture, debt as a form of indenture, banking practices as an extreme form of usury, and increasing references to debt jubilees. This rhetoric belongs to the ancient and not-so-ancient past, but today debt extraction is a primary means of accumulation among the creditor class. This debt bondage has a very real psychological impact; individuals in debt feel it's a life sentence that is foreclosing their future. In a very literal sense, the more debt you take on, the more you are pledging the wages of the future to your creditor. That sense of the future being swallowed up is one of the most common psychological impacts of taking on a large debt load.

Hoekstra: The Occupy movement's Rolling Jubilee project bought up and abolished personal debt. This "bailout of the people by the people" abolished $15 million of personal debt by spending only $400,000 to purchase that debt. How does that work?

Ross: The Rolling Jubilee is a project that I have been very involved in, a project of Strike Debt!, a debt-resistance program that is an offshoot of Occupy. It's a very simple idea: Through crowdfunding, we raised a lot of money over a short time because people really like this idea. We used this money to buy distressed debt, which gets sold on the secondary debt marketplace. Banks and creditors are obliged to move nonperforming loans off their books in 90 days, and this distressed debt gets sold very, very cheaply—for pennies on the dollar—to debt buyers. These buyers then sell it on to collection agencies who come after you, the debtor, to try to collect the full amount of debt after having paid only a pittance for it. Our idea was to buy some of this debt very cheaply. We decided to focus on medical debt, as no one should have to go into debt for becoming sick, and instead of collecting on the debt after we bought it, we simply abolished it or forgave it. We wrote to the debtors telling them that they're off the hook.

Initially, we were told that we would get a ratio of about 20 to 1. In other words, that for every dollar we spent, we could abolish $20 worth of debt. We managed to get 50 to 1 ratios for recent buys and have been able to stretch the dollars much further. For us it is a public education project, an opportunity to educate the public about the shadowy operations of the secondary debt market. Now, if your collection agent calls you up and you know that they pay very little money for the debt, you're going to have a very different conversation with that collection agency. For other people, the sheer demonstration of the fact that you can abolish debt so simply, especially through a mutual aid project, was a real eye-opener. So it accomplished what we set out to do—to help out some people. Several thousand people's debt was forgiven or abolished, but more importantly we educated the public about how the really shadowy, murky debt marketplace works.

Hoekstra: Morality and debt seem to be deeply and historically intertwined in that there's a collective social sense that it's unconscionable to avoid repayment. Your book seems to turn that on its head, saying it's actually the current system of debt that's immoral.

Ross: Yes, that is certainly something I urge in the book, to turn around these accusations and the moralism that the finance industry usually trains on debtors and point it at the finance industry itself. With evidence of widespread predatory, deceitful, and fraudulent conduct of the big banks, we need to ask, "Who is really the delinquent agent on the debt landscape? Which entity is the moral hazard to society?" In most cases, it's not the small debtor who cannot pay back debt. The delinquent one is the creditor who preys upon debtors, when it's quite obvious they will never be able to pay back their debt, and who then lies and cheats in order to enforce repayments. "Payback morality" is one of the most effective instruments that the finance industry has for collecting profit, and this morality runs very deep. It's been and still is considered taboo to think about not repaying your debt.

However, in the wake of the 2008 financial crash, a double standard was exposed. The big banks were really not expected to pay back their debts at all. They got government bailouts, while the small debtors were the ones still expected to pay back their debts. More and more people have become aware of this double standard, and as a result, payback moralism has eroded somewhat over the years.

Hoekstra: One of the goals of your book is to make a case for debt refusal, to call for a debtors' movement. What would that look like? Are there alternatives to our current system of credit and debt?

Ross: We know there is an appetite out there for a debtors' movement that has been actively building for a few years now, and we know that this movement is necessary because current levels of indebtedness are a threat to democracy. I wrote *Creditocracy* to provide some arguments for debt repudiation or debt refusal. The arguments draw very heavily from the Jubilee South movement, a movement very active in the 1990s and 2000s that has tried, with some success, to get the external debts of developing countries forgiven or repudiated. My book, however, focuses on household debts in the Global North because the "debt trap" conditions that were imposed on developing countries in the 1960s and '70s have now moved into the North. The big shift we've seen in recent decades is that debt affects almost every consumer household in the North now. My book argues that the time is right to apply some of the arguments of the international jubilee movement to personal debt. A successful debtors' movement has to figure out ways of threatening mass default on a collective basis in order to gain some leverage over the financial industry.

Hoekstra: Speaking of international debt movements, how does climate change and the climate justice movement fit in with this for you? How are discussions of debt and climate change linked?

Ross: The book tries to make a case for distinguishing between debts that are illegitimate and debts that are legitimate, which debts should be honored and which debts should be refused. Most climate debts should be honored. The most interesting thing is that the nature of climate debt reverses the typical structure of credit. [Countries in the Global] North are usually the creditors, and the Southern countries are the debtors. In this case, climate debt is the exact opposite. The rich countries are the debtors. . . .

There are all sorts of ways to calculate these debts, most often measured against accumulated ecological debt from centuries of colonial extraction. One of the big challenges is to figure out how to get the rich countries to acknowledge their debt. They usually think of them in terms of aid and talk about them in terms of climate aid, rather than debt or reparations, which has different legal consequences. Let's just say that they do acknowledge them, then how would the payments be distributed in an equitable fashion? This is one of the big challenges in the climate justice movement. Also, how do we ensure that the debt payments actually would get circulated and distributed to the people who need it most and are most affected? But climate debts in general are a complicated and complicating factor on the landscape of debt.

Although I think we should be in the position of refusing a lot of debt, that is one that should be honored. We should figure out how our governments and also how the chief polluting industries and the high carbon beneficiaries should be held responsible for paying that debt.

PARTICIPANT PROFILE

Andrew Ross is in the department of social and cultural analysis at New York University. He is a scholar-activist working on labor, urban studies, and environmental justice.

8

of carbon and cash

ERIN HOEKSTRA

As Andrew Ross told us in the previous chapter, climate debt refers to the harmful carbon emissions created by countries like the United States and the grave effects that climate change is having on poorer, developing countries in the Global South. First introduced in the United Nations Framework Convention on Climate Change, the concept of *climate debt* has motivated politicians, scientists, academics, and advocates to look closely at how climate change is experienced by rich and poor countries. Climate debt, for them, represents another example of the persistent global inequality between the developed countries in the Global North and the developing countries of the Global South. Social scientists are playing an important part in documenting the social movements around climate debt and in developing methods to calculate and account for such debts.

Meanwhile, this persistent global inequality serves as the basis for several international debt-relief movements. For instance, the Jubilee movement, predicated on the biblical notion of the "jubilee" (when debts were forgiven every seventh year), is a global movement based in Britain and other Global North countries that advocates for forgiving and abolishing the debts that Global South countries supposedly owe from the colonial era. In this instance, the "creditors" are wealthy, developed nations that once colonized and extracted resources like gold, oil, coal, and diamonds from countries they later charged with "debt repayment." In one alarming example, Haiti was forced to pay the French government from 1825 to 1947 to compensate for "property" lost to French slave owners when Haitian slaves successfully revolted. The Jubilee movement uses the debt-abolishment argument to pressure countries to forgive such debt rather than force other nations into bankruptcy. The Jubilee movement has had some limited success, but wealthy countries continue to pressure poorer countries to pay outstanding debts.

The climate debt and climate justice movements share some similarities with the Jubilee movement: Both are based on the persistence and injustice of global inequality, both recognize that the high consumption in wealthier countries hurts poorer countries, and both force us to consider the nature of legitimate and illegitimate debts. Like the Jubilee movement, the broader concept of ecological debt, under which climate debt falls, draws from the legacy of the ecological exploitation of colonized countries. Andrew Simms draws out this similarity in *Ecological Debt: Global Warming and the Wealth of Nations* (Pluto Press, 2009), arguing that in both climate debt and international debt, those who have played the smallest role in creating the problems have borne the greatest burdens. Those most responsible for climate crises have skirted responsibility.

from debt to reparations

Climate debt is predicated on the idea that all countries and all humanity share the environment and the earth's atmosphere, a sort of "global commons" according to Simms. If all nations and people have an equal claim to this global commons, then the countries and people who are overusing and even damaging the environment are racking up an ecological debt to the wider community and should have to account for the consequences of their behavior. In the instance of climate change, this debt comprises greenhouse gases and CO_2 accruing in the atmosphere. The climate justice movement focuses on reparations for countries that are experiencing the harshest effects of climate change, brought on by the emissions of other countries. At the same time, it also tries to eradicate the debt (or these harmful emissions) altogether.

In Ross's interview and in his book *Creditocracy*, he distinguishes between legitimate and illegitimate debts and argues that climate debt is one legitimate debt that should be repaid. Whereas the Jubilee movement draws on a framework of debt forgiveness of illegitimate foreign debts, the climate debt movement turns the tables from the South to the North and is based on the more radical notion of reparations. Unlike discourses of "international aid," which emphasize the benevolence of the donor country, the language of reparations recognizes that an injury or injustice has occurred for which restitution is necessary. Germany paid reparations to Holocaust victims after World War II, for instance, and in the United States, descendants of slaves have long argued for compensation for the enslavement of their ancestors. By framing climate debt alongside these clear instances of harm done to the less powerful, Global South countries and their advocates demand recognition of the unequal creation and consequences of climate change.

Notoriously difficult to quantify, climate debt is measured in numerous ways but is usually divided into two elements: emissions and adaptation debt. Emissions debt refers to the overproduction of emissions that diminish the earth's capacity to absorb greenhouse gases. Adaptation debt addresses the costs associated with the adverse effects of these emissions. In "Climate Debt: A Primer," Matthew Stilwell argues that adaptation debt is associated with "the escalating losses, damages, and lost development opportunities facing developing countries." Within climate debt, emissions debt is the most easily quantified since, Ross explains, it "*can* be measured more reliably, on the basis of atmospheric emissions estimates." The carbon debt of the overemitting countries is then calculated at $100 per ton of CO_2.

If a "carbon quota" were allocated to countries on a per capita basis, the biggest emissions offenders would rack up a carbon debt. Those (usually poorer) countries that create fewer emissions than their quota would then receive a carbon credit.

the debt of history

The question about how to calculate these values complicates the measuring of carbon debt by country. Should the debt, for instance, be determined by a country's *current* emissions levels? Should it take into account cumulative emissions from a given moment in history until today? The rationale for using cumulative emissions draws from historical and social scientific research that finds that countries almost inevitably increase their emissions as they develop infrastructure and industry. Calculating this debt from current emissions levels would clearly disadvantage developing countries like China and India that have not *historically* had high emissions levels but have increased carbon production with recent development. At the same time, using current emissions levels would excuse or minimize charges to historical emissions offenders—developed countries like the United States that have already built infrastructure and industry.

Should countries actually follow through with repayment of climate debts, the next question is, of course, how these funds would be distributed not only across countries facing the most drastic effects of climate change, but also *within* these countries to ensure that the individuals who have lost their homes or livelihoods as a result of events like natural disasters and drought receive the needed assistance.

It may seem unrealistic to expect wealthy nations to suddenly fork over billions of dollars in climate reparations, but the *concept* of climate debt is proving powerful in making claims on the world stage and raising awareness of the differential effects of climate change across countries. Sociologists studying international debt and reparations are analyzing these debates even as they help frame them.

Per Capita Fossil-Fuel CO_2 Emission Rates, 2010

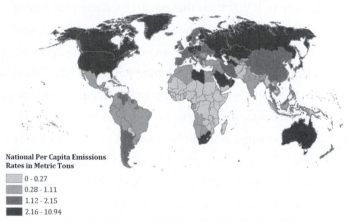

National Per Capita Emissions Rates in Metric Tons

- 0 - 0.27
- 0.28 - 1.11
- 1.12 - 2.15
- 2.16 - 10.94

Source: Boden, T.A., G. Marland, and R.J. Andres. 2012. Global, Regional, and National Fossil-Fuel CO2 Emissions. Carbon Dioxide Information Analysis Center, Oak Ridge National Laboratory, U.S. Department of Energy, Oak Ridge, Tenn., U.S.A. Graphic created for TheSocietyPages.org by Suzy McElrath

Cumulative Fossil Fuel CO_2 Emissions by Source Region, 1751–2012

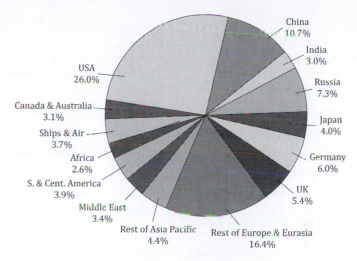

China
10.7%

India
3.0%

USA
26.0%

Russia
7.3%

Canada & Australia
3.1%

Japan
4.0%

Ships & Air
3.7%

Germany
6.0%

Africa
2.6%

S. & Cent. America
3.9%

UK
5.4%

Middle East
3.4%

Rest of Asia Pacific
4.4%

Rest of Europe & Eurasia
16.4%

Source: Boden, T.A., G. Marland, and R.J. Andres. 2012. Global, Regional, and National Fossil-Fuel CO2 Emissions.
Carbon Dioxide Information Analysis Center, Oak Ridge National Laboratory, U.S. Department of Energy, Oak Ridge, Tenn., U.S.A.
Graphic created for TheSocietyPages.org by Suzy McElrath

Annual Fossil Fuel CO_2 Emissions by Source Region, 2012

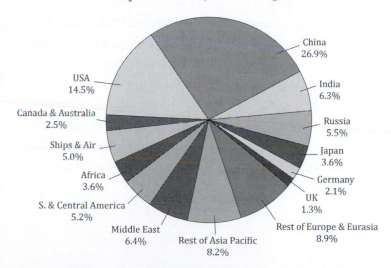

China
26.9%

USA
14.5%

India
6.3%

Canada & Australia
2.5%

Russia
5.5%

Ships & Air
5.0%

Japan
3.6%

Africa
3.6%

Germany
2.1%

S. & Central America
5.2%

UK
1.3%

Middle East
6.4%

Rest of Asia Pacific
8.2%

Rest of Europe & Eurasia
8.9%

Source: Boden, T.A., G. Marland, and R.J. Andres. 2012. Global, Regional, and National Fossil-Fuel CO2 Emissions.
Carbon Dioxide Information Analysis Center, Oak Ridge National Laboratory, U.S. Department of Energy, Oak Ridge, Tenn., U.S.A.
Graphic created for TheSocietyPages.org by Suzy McElrath

RECOMMENDED READING

Niclas Hällström. 2012. *What Next Volume III: Climate, Development and Equity.* Uppsala, Sweden: Dag Hammarskjöld Foundation and the What Next Forum. Offers a great primer on climate debt, explaining the severity of climate change and the movement for climate justice and equity.

Andrew K. Jorgenson. 2014. "Economic development and the carbon intensity of human well-being," *Nature Climate Change* 4:186–189. Examines the relationship between development and carbon emissions and analyzes Africa as the exception to this rule.

Naomi Klein. 2009. "Climate Rage," *Rolling Stone,* Nov. 12. Explains the politics behind and main actors in the climate debt movement.

Andrew Ross. 2014. *Creditocracy and the Case for Debt Refusal.* New York: OR Books. Locates climate debt within a wider examination of various types of "legitimate" and "illegitimate" debt.

Kirk R. Smith. 1996. "The Natural Debt: North and South," in *Climate Change: Developing Southern Hemisphere Perspectives* (pp. 423–448), edited by Thomas W. Giambelluca and Anne Henderson-Sellers. Chichester, UK: John Wiley and Sons. Examines the unequal effects of climate change from the perspective of the Global South.

TSP tie-in

the not-so-alternative media picture

Experiencing debt is one thing, but being portrayed as a deadbeat or a failure is quite another. With so much media attention paid to debt and financial crises, we sometimes forget the human beings behind the headlines. And imagine how much salt is added to displaced homeowners' wounds when they're labeled "financially illiterate" or "ignorant" after losing their houses to foreclosure on a shady mortgage deal.

People of color have historically turned to alternative media for "counternarratives" to such portrayals. But, as journalism professor Catherine Squires has pointed out, even black-oriented media like *Black Enterprise* and TheRoot.com told the story of the United States' subprime mortgage crisis in much the same way as the dominant press. Blacks and Latinos thus came under scrutiny from media outlets supposedly representative of their experiences as people of color.

The black press once offered sharp institutional critiques of free-market capitalism, racism, and imperialism, but Squires finds that it now emphasizes individuals' bad choices—just like the mainstream press. Sociologist Amin Ghaziani suggests that this focus on individualized, rather than collective, problems is a product of our current era of "proliferating posts" (i.e., postfeminist, postracial, postgay). Earlier counternarratives to racism and imperialism, in contrast, represented direct threats to arguments that depicted the individual as the perpetrator of his or her own plight. More generally, Squires and other critical media scholars are showing the rise of neoliberal and postracial discourse in the alternative press. In the case of the subprime mortgage crisis, these stories of individual responsibility and a color-blind society obscured the role of redlining, fraudulent loan practices, and discriminatory rate setting affecting black and Latino borrowers.

Alternative media outlets have long helped to pick up the slack of mainstream institutions that fail to adequately represent the views and opinions of all. If the racially and economically marginalized cannot rely on alternative media outlets to defend them, whom do they turn to? As this volume's Changing Lenses feature reminds us, sometimes friends willing to loan us $1 are much more generous than the bank fronting us $50,000.

—RAHSAAN MAHADEO

critical takes

9

economic decline and the american dream

KEVIN LEICHT

The 2008–2010 recession in the United States was the worst since the Great Depression of the 1930s. Millions of jobs were lost. Trillions of dollars in wealth evaporated. The Bush and Obama administrations put together emergency measures designed to prevent total financial collapse, with the hope that economic health would quickly return. But when social scientists take a closer look at what constitutes "economic health" for most Americans, it's a bit like claiming your Uncle George looks "good" because he isn't dead. The problems revealed by the recession took years to come to a head. There were plenty of signals that the American dream was in trouble, but they were covered up by the easy availability of credit that was artificially driving economic growth and middle-class prosperity.

the scale of the problem

The recession numbers are staggering, and the human costs incalculable. World markets lost $50 trillion in 2008 alone, roughly $8,300 for every person on earth. The United States lost around 7 million jobs, and the federal budget deficit is slated to hit $1.2 trillion by the end of 2014. The Bush and Obama administrations assembled a bank bailout worth $770 billion and a $15 billion bailout package for Chrysler and GM, two of our "Big Three" automakers that employ hundreds of thousands of Americans. Home prices (the major source of wealth for most middle-class Americans) dropped 20% in nine years and, according to the Federal Reserve, it could take at least another decade to recover to prerecession levels. Commercial real estate vacancies are running as high as 20% in many major cities. And consumer demand and confidence (measured monthly by the University of Michigan) haven't been this low since the early 1970s.

The conditions of the so-called recovery may be more chilling: record high corporate profits and anemic job creation. The following graphic shows corporate profits as a percentage of the gross domestic product in the United States, with shaded areas indicating recession years. While corporate profits hit another peak in 2012, job creation has been so slow that it will be many years before employment even matches

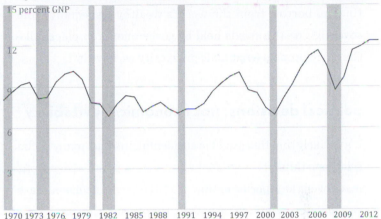

Corporate Profits as a Percentage of Gross Domestic Product, 1970–2013

Source: U.S. Census Bureau, Current Population Survey, Annual Social and Economic Supplements.
Notes: 2012 dollars.
Graphic created for TheSocietyPages.org by Suzy McElrath

2007 levels. Steady jobs at steady wages, the very staple of middle-class life, are elusive. The official unemployment rate seems to be stuck around 7%, but the more inclusive "U-6" rate is more than 13%. This includes discouraged and other "marginally attached" workers and those forced to work part-time because they can't find full-time jobs.

The pain is not uniformly shared. The crisis of the middle class in particular can be seen in record numbers of foreclosures, bankruptcies, and loan defaults. The inability to maintain the accoutrements of a middle-class life has stalled social mobility. The United States now has the lowest rate of social mobility of any industrialized nation. And we continue to borrow from the world's wealthy (especially from sovereign wealth funds held by governments in places like China) to prop up what little prosperity we have left.

political decisions, not economic inevitability

It's unlikely that this plight is accidental. Instead, many social scientists think it's a product of a series of political decisions made over a long period of time. Together, these decisions have rigged the economic game to favor the already affluent.

For one, our tax system was changed to dramatically favor unearned income (such as capital gains) and disfavor or tax earned income through the federal income tax, the federal payroll tax that pays for Social Security and Medicare, and regressive state and local taxes that take a larger percentage of the incomes of the poor and middle classes than they do the wealthy. This trend began with Reagan-era tax cuts and continued through the 2004 Bush tax cut that remains a major subject of debate. We've hindered the ability of workers to unionize, and union contracts set standards for the rest of the economy (regardless of whether individuals are union members). And, as the furor over Mitt Romney's tax returns during the 2012 presidential campaign makes clear, we've turned tax avoidance into a national pastime for the affluent.

A once-overblown statement by the incredibly wealthy Leona Helmsley—"Taxes are only for the little people"—is now actually true.

Rigging the political game to favor the already wealthy has occurred at multiple levels, many of them unseen by average Americans going about the business of finding work and raising families. We've allowed affluent investors to move investments and jobs overseas to lower costs. We've favored investments through the tax system at the expense of earned income. Then, to make up for the revenue the federal government doesn't collect to pay for the programs we say we want, we've sold these same affluent people treasury bills at favorable interest rates to pay for what the government does—in effect, a tax with a rebate attached to it. (Wouldn't you like to pay taxes now and get all your tax money back, plus interest, in 20 years? Sounds good to me!) We've allowed investors to import goods made overseas to sell to American consumers at lower prices, and, in the process of doing all of this, we've increased the revenues investors receive.

Yet the wealthy claim to do their part as "makers" who create jobs. They loan our governments money (but skirt taxes), hire employees and build headquarters (but engage in activities that lower individual earnings), and loan consumers money (to replace lost earnings and help keep up with the middle-class lifestyle). Each of these tradeoffs benefits wealthy individuals and corporations. This situation is so unfair that James Galbraith at the Lyndon Johnson School of Public Affairs at the University of Texas claims the United States now has three welfare states—a meagerly funded welfare state for the poor, a privately funded welfare state tied to employment for some segments of the middle class, and an interest/rent payment welfare state for the world's wealthy.

avoiding the issues

More interesting still is the American political system's reaction to claims that our economic and political systems are rigged to favor the already wealthy. Movements like Occupy Wall Street and "We are the 99%" emerged to make this very point, but the response from pundits and politicians is what Scott Fitzgerald and I call "the politics of displacement."

The politics of displacement is meeting every question about money and fairness with a screaming match about anything, *anything*, but money. As David Brock points out in his book *The Republican Noise Machine* (Crown, 2004), any topic will do: Let's talk about abortion, school prayer, flag burning, gun rights, gay marriage, fluoridated water, Sharia law in Oklahoma, or Obama's birthplace. Anything will do so long as it distracts from talk of money and fairness. Right-wing talk radio would be nothing without the politics of displacement

(I once challenged a former Republican congressman to give an example of "mutuality" by directing me to left-wing hate radio on the AM dial—he stood in front of hundreds, flummoxed).

Many of our citizens totally buy into the politics of displacement (luckily, not as many as pundits think). If they are going downhill, the argument goes, somebody must be to blame: blacks, Hispanics, gays, liberals, the media, or academics! The possibility that we were economically duped by the people we voted into office simply because they gave voice to our cultural prejudices doesn't seem to occur to many.

Several reasons—obviously, they are not mutually exclusive—allow the politics of displacement to distract us. First, we let it happen. As voters, Americans have let our political parties and candidates avoid questions of economic fairness or deflect them in directions that lead to greater division, cynicism, and passivity. There is fighting in professional hockey because the rules permit it and it works; the same is true in politics.

Second, campaign donors and corporate sponsors are weary of politicians who want to vigorously fight social inequality. Issues of opportunity are best addressed, for this audience, as opportunities not taken, not as nonexistent opportunities. Some campaign donors, like single-issue interest groups, actually play into the politics of displacement. If lots of voters are mobilized around issues that don't involve money, presto! You can have a successful campaign in the middle of a recession, and it won't address money at all.

The two-party, winner-take-all political system is the third reason a politics of displacement can continue. It has produced what political commentator Kevin Phillips has long described as "the world's most enthusiastic capitalist party" (the GOP) and "the world's second most enthusiastic capitalist party" (the Democratic Party). Both parties make transient appeals to middle-class and sometimes even poor voters, but both are funded by wealthy capitalists. The only real difference between two parties of economic elites is their acceptance of twenty-first-century cultural trends. Democrats focus on the professional upper-middle-class, high-technology entrepreneurs, and other victors in the new knowledge economy, offering economic redistribution that favors a new elite and cultural ideas that alienate the middle and working classes. Republicans pitch to traditional business classes, Wall Street investors, and business elites in traditional industries, as well as those who believe there is a "culture war" in America—that moral degeneration is the major cause of declining economic prospects.

Assuming both parties will harm the average citizen's economic picture, why *wouldn't* voters go for the party that best reflects their cultural values and emotional issues? One group *might* give you a job and pay you a living wage, but they're educated elites from diverse cultural backgrounds. The other group won't give you a job at all or pay you minimum wage, but they're white guys with families and children—they simply *look* more like their voter base.

Fourth, the spin cycle of the media nearly demands a politics of displacement. Cable television and 24-hour talk radio need topics and conflict if they are to keep pulling the audiences their advertisers pay for. U.S. media spend endless hours delineating the virtuous "we" and the unworthy "they," each framed as it best appeals to the outlet's audience. Conservative media will place blame for "our" problems on "them"—every conceivable group that isn't wealthy, white, heterosexual, or Christian. Liberal media will place blame for "our" problems on "them"—every conceivable group that isn't highly educated, highly tolerant, and highly urban. Each insists that their representation of the divisions of American life is correct, logical, and deserving of trust.

Finally, economic segregation allows for a politics of displacement. We can avoid the issues because we surround ourselves with people like us. In the United States, economic segregation prevents us from empathizing with those who are less fortunate because they are often invisible to us. They don't live in our part of town, or we meet them as waitstaff in the low-wage service industry. "They" look like us, but we hardly realize they may be from drastically different economic circumstances than we are. Gated communities, high-rise condominiums, and suburbs have contributed mightily to this silo effect. It's hard to care about those we can't see. Our own needs will always seem most important until we branch out.

To their credit, some members of the press, public, and even political circles are picking up on the cynical politics of displacement, and there are hopeful signs of change on the political landscape.

moving forward

If much of what we've seen and experienced is the result of conscious political choices, the remedies must come in the form of different political choices. Many writers talk about the effect that big money, wealthy patrons, and corporate donors have on politics. The Citizens United decision that allows corporations to make political donations as if they were individuals and the Supreme Court decision invalidating contribution limits by individual donors certainly do not reduce the influence of the wealthy.

One way to redistribute income and continue to promote investment-based capitalism would be to widen our participation in it. Right now, almost all unearned income from interest earnings and investments is bottled up in the top 10% to

15% of the wealth distribution. The bottom half of the distribution owns nothing. Providing each child with an individual investment account at birth ($10,000 or so), managed by the government in the same way payroll tax revenues are invested, would allow the wonders of compound interest to do their work. Starting your adult life with $50,000 would mean the ability to pay off college loans, start a small business, make a down payment on a house, or move to a part of the country where there are better job opportunities. If the money isn't needed right away, young adults could just add to their individual investment account slowly as they enter the full-time workforce. In any case, the availability of a small store of wealth from which adult life could be started would make a world of difference and cost the rest of us surprisingly little.

A second way forward requires more coordinated action. We've allowed our political system to substantially reward investors who speculate with our money, destroy jobs, outsource production and services, and otherwise interfere with our lives in ways that are ultimately destructive to the larger culture and community. Instead of cutting taxes on unearned incomes and then waiting for a "supply-side miracle"—tax cuts that would stimulate the economy enough to bring a big windfall in revenue for the government and rising wages for everyone else—why not make the miracle explicit? Tie the capital gains tax rate on investment income to the real earn-

ings for families of four. If real earnings move upward, capital gains tax rates go down and investors get a rebate. If real
earnings stagnate or move downward, capital gains tax rates
go up. If incomes remain static, capital gains tax rates continue to go up. Tying the accumulation of wealth to the economic well-being of the rest of us would alter the incentives
that wealthy Americans and most investors face and, perhaps, restart the virtuous cycle of rising consumption from
rising incomes.

A third way forward is for voters to pay attention to our
candidates and their promises. Ask direct questions about
monetary policy. Ask for clarification when you don't understand the answers. Demand follow-through and ignore out-
bursts of cultural prejudice that seem like flimsy ways to
redirect attention.

We can afford such steps to reinvigorate the American
dream. We will *all* be better off when we take them.

RECOMMENDED READING

Jacob S. Hacker and Paul Pierson. 2010. *Winner-Take-All Politics:
How Washington Made the Rich Richer—and Turned Its Back
on the Middle Class*. New York: Simon & Schuster. Tells the

story of how American politics created today's enormous economic inequalities.

Kevin T. Leicht and Scott T. Fitzgerald. 2007. *Postindustrial Peasants: The Illusion of Middle-Class Prosperity*. New York: Worth Publishers. Documents the recent struggles of the American middle class, drawing connections to peasants in feudal societies and sharecroppers in agrarian societies.

Katherine Porter (ed). 2012. *Broke: How Debt Bankrupts the Middle Class*. Stanford, CA: Stanford University Press. A diverse and powerful collection of research based on the 2007 Consumer Bankruptcy Project.

are some universities too big to fail?

ERIC BEST

student debt, for-profit education, and the federal government

According to the Department of Education (ED), for-profit universities educate about 12% of college students, yet these students are responsible for about half of student loan defaults. Increasingly, these institutions are under legal attack from former students, state regulators, and even the Department of Justice. The obvious solution is to sanction or shut down the most flagrant debt-for-diploma mills, but the reticence to take such steps brings to light another, more disturbing issue: the federal government would have to forgive federal loan debt from schools that shut down or lose accreditation.

In today's lexicon, "too big to fail" usually refers to companies that are large in size or market share, but that's not what's key. A firm actually becomes "too big to fail" when it achieves a level of importance that discourages regulators from stopping its bad behavior. For-profit universities are now some of the nation's largest educational institutions (in terms of enrollment numbers and student loan obligations), but some may also be too big to fail. Students at some of the largest for-profit universities now have so much outstanding loan debt that shutting down the institutions might be more painful to federal regulating bodies than simply allowing the universities to continue. Because of their prolific growth and massive size, the ED now has a financial disincentive to shut down or remove accreditation from these schools. That is, fear of a massive potential write-down is protecting some of the largest for-profit universities' access to federal student loans.

for-profit boom (and the coming bust)

The American education market is changing. Critics attack the commercialization of education, with its focus on earning potential after graduation ("return on investment") over the pursuit of knowledge before graduation. But the commercialization starts earlier—at the recruitment stage. The business is more about increasing enrollment numbers and tuition dollars than personalized education decisions, meaning the worst offenders are for-profit institutions that promise democratized educations to all. No longer limited to trade schools and providers of part-time graduate degrees, for-profit institutions bombard potential students with print and media advertising and direct them to online and accelerated educational programs. This unconventional educational format is in many ways a race to the bottom, with institutions competing for the shortest degree completion times, most lenient instructors, and most flexible schedules. Despite this, for-profits offering these amenities are likely here to stay, and their presence has created a stratified educational system. Prospective students can choose from exclusive, expensive, and demanding full-time programs or for-profit systems that promise fast, real-world education and part-time study. As traditional universities attempt to become more prestigious and for-profit schools fight to offer the easiest path to a degree, the educational journeys they offer grow ever farther apart.

Five of the 10 schools with the highest amounts of total outstanding student loan debt are for-profit universities with electronic distance-learning programs. Educating students online allows universities to offer degree programs that are not limited by geography or time of day, and often do not require additional faculty hires. These programs are now much larger than traditional colleges, and their total loan amounts will continue to grow faster.

The real worry about online for-profit education isn't actually a lack of quality instruction, but the simultaneous lack of marketable degrees and the reality of student loan debt. Many for-profit schools began in the second half of the twentieth century as niche schools—niches, though, are not typically sustainable high-growth areas, and for-profit schools now run national campaigns directing prospective students to online portals and marketing themselves as replacements for traditional college and community college educations. They concentrate on reaching student populations such as first-generation college students, older students, and college dropouts, promising experiential programs and easily obtained degrees. In doing so, they became more expensive, less specialized, and more aggressive in recruitment. As their investors demand growth, these institutions attempt to convince more and more students that the value of a college education is enormous and any amount of debt is worth the panache of a college diploma. These sales tactics, coupled with exploding tuition costs and vulnerable student populations, have created universities financed almost exclusively by government loans.

is the phoenix a canary?

The growth of education loans is actually representative of changing attitudes towards debt in the United States. From 1999 to 2009, college tuitions grew about 32% (accounting for inflation). This change did not occur in a vacuum. Buoyed by access to more credit cards, home equity loans, and college loans, and a cultural attitude about "good" debt, demand for college education rose alongside prices. Benefiting from this era of broadband Internet, increased debt tolerance, and a strong demand for education, for-profit universities experienced a banner decade that is not likely to be repeated.

But unconventional schools often seem to end in disaster: new competitors come to market, tastes change. So far, only small for-profit schools have shut down or lost accreditation; the subsequent loan forgiveness amounts have gone unnoticed, absorbed by the greater economy. Further, forgiving loans seems like a good idea, the right thing to do: Students enter a program under the assumption that they will be able to obtain a degree, and if they are unable to complete their education because the school collapses, it seems only fair that loans taken out to obtain a product that no longer exists should be forgiven. Those students who do complete their degrees only to see their alma mater collapse are left with an education deemed worthless or lacking credibility; they suffer in the job market, so we can easily justify forgiving their loans. All of this is to say, in the past, trade schools and small for-profit universities failed without really drawing attention. Now that's nearly impossible. For-profit online universities are the whales of the student loan debt market. The University of Phoenix holds the honor of the highest amount of total student debt at a single institution. With student loan debt in the billions, the largest for-profit universities may very well be too big to fail.

Paradoxically, these institutions are also far too big to succeed. Education is clearly not a priority; the aforementioned giant, University of Phoenix, has a six-year bachelor's degree graduation rate of only 9% according to the Education Trust, far below traditional universities and its for-profit peers. Graduation rates at some for-profit programs are so dismal that many states' attorneys general and the Department of Justice are examining their practices.

In many ways, the University of Phoenix is the canary in the coal mine. While the institution is extremely large, the important numbers are all about growth rates. Before the school experienced massive growth, the ED attempted to improve behavior at the University of Phoenix with lawsuits in 2003, audits in 2004, and program reviews afterward. By 2010, though, the ED had seemingly stopped overseeing the University of Phoenix; investors and the public were no longer aware of ED actions against the university. This is likely the result of an awkward stalemate: If the government shuts down the University of Phoenix, the ED may be on the hook for billions of dollars in loan forgiveness. Doing anything to undermine the credibility of these universities might lead to a loss of accreditation or their closure, and then all the loans to all the students would have to be forgiven at the federal level. The massive potential write-down can't be ignored in considering the ED's passivity toward delinquent for-profit universities, but it's not a prudent long-term strategy. Each year these universities remain open, loan amounts compound. Make no mistake: These universities cannot sustain growth rates that will satisfy corporate investors forever. Having saturated the market, growth rates at the largest for-profit universities are slowing and share prices are falling. Some of these institutions will collapse on their own.

Several for-profit universities, including the University of Phoenix, are already flirting with disaster. The government mandates that no more than 90% of an institution's loan dollars can come from federal loans. Instead of lowering tuition or providing other methods of payment, some for-profits chose to raise tuition beyond federal reimbursement levels, forcing students to pay by other means. The University of Phoenix also has a history of returning all federal loans for some students who drop out, in an attempt to keep default numbers acceptable. The university then privately sues students for back tuition.

Despite inquiries into for-profit universities at Senate Health, Education, Labor, and Pensions (HELP) Committee hearings, Congress created loopholes in 2008 to allow these universities to count some federal money (such as GI Bill payments) against their 90% federal borrowing cap. That is, every returning veteran enrolled by a for-profit university allows that school to recruit nine other students paying the entirety of their tuition with federal loans. Generally, the government appears complicit in allowing for-profit universities to function for as long as possible with as many federally backed loans as necessary.

The ED is likely reluctant to confront this issue for the same reason that banks, mortgage lenders, and the Federal Reserve were seemingly oblivious to their financial ills: The embarrassment of admitting we are in an unsustainable situation is apparently greater than the savings from calling the bluff now. Every year we wait to admit there is a crisis in the student loan industry, things will get worse. There is no one fall guy, and everyone will get hurt when the charade ends.

what's a government to do?

If the government denies federal loans to for-profit universities like the University of Phoenix, they will instantly be exposed for their unsustainable business models and shut their doors. The government will be left holding the tab. If the ED encourages accreditation organizations to deny renewals to for-profit universities, those schools will ultimately fail. The same is true for limiting the number of new students who can enroll in these universities; if for-profit institutions stop getting new tuition dollars or downsize too rapidly, they will fail. Because of loan forgiveness laws already in place, it is impossible for the federal government to take a strong negative stance on for-profit education without losing a significant amount of money almost immediately.

So, while some individuals and states have seen the light, calling for an end to for-profit education, the federal government has a short-term financial incentive to keep the degrees granted by these educations valid. These institutions continue functioning even though regulators know they are a bad deal for students and taxpayers. For instance, even though former students of for-profit universities are defaulting on loans in unprecedented numbers, right now their debt isn't forgiven; the onus is on the borrower, since personal bankruptcy will not eliminate many federal student loan obligations. The government, then, is publicly claiming that bankrupt students will repay their debts but is privately aware that repayment is unlikely and the expense will eventually fall to the federal government. Anecdotal examples of graduates failing to launch in the face of staggering debt now appear frequently in popular news outlets, and the idea of just abandoning loan payments in the vein of strategic mortgage default is gaining traction.

Short-term write-downs, though, are no excuse for silence as hundreds of thousands of students are aggressively sold, persuaded, or downright duped into career-long debt and taxpayers are left liable for these loans after almost inevitable defaults. Enrollment at for-profit schools is dropping and loan defaults are rising, but the real costs to the government and taxpayers will not be realized until the schools lose accreditation or shut their doors. Based on the potential legal action led by classes of students, investors, and states, it seems it's only a matter of time before the ED's hand is forced. The reality is that both the for-profit education and student loan systems are fundamentally broken, and sooner we fix them, the better. Fixing this system is going to be expensive, disruptive, and deeply unpopular. We will all end up paying for this slow but huge mistake. But when the largest for-profit educational institutions are too big to fail and too big to succeed, something has to be done.

RECOMMENDED READING

Eric Best. 2012. "Debt and the American Dream," *Society* 49(4):349–352. Discusses the ways in which the mortgage debt crisis may serve as a template for a coming student loan debt crisis.

Rachel E. Dwyer, Laura McCloud, and Randy Hodson. 2012. "Debt and Graduation from American Universities," *Social Forces* 90(4):1133–1155. Considers student debt as both a "useful resource for making needed investments" and a harness that may increase vulnerabilities and limit options.

Anya Kamenetz. 2006. *Generation Debt.* New York: Riverhead Books. The subtitle says it all: *How Our Future Was Sold Out for Student Loans, Bad Jobs, No Benefits, and Tax Cuts for Rich Geezers—and How to Fight Back.* See also Kamenetz's latest book, *DIY U* (Chelsea Green, 2010), on an educational reformation.

Janet Lorin. 2012. "Students Pay SLM 9.25% on Exploitative Loans for College," *Bloomberg News* (June 4). A detailed reading of payday-loan-style tactics in student lending.

Andrew Martin and Andrew W. Lehren. 2012. "A Generation Hobbled by the Soaring Cost of College," *New York Times* (May 12). A great overview of student loan debt and the individuals facing it.

Stanford University's Center for Education Policy Analysis (cepa.stanford.edu). This website is a constantly updated treasure trove of informative publications and accessible research on the conundrum of contemporary education.

pension fund capitalism
with g. william domhoff

RAHSAAN MAHADEO

"When is a debt not a debt? When the money is promised to prospective pensioners." So wrote the *Economist* in 2013, as Poland's government overhauled its pension system to reduce public debt. Closer to home, Detroit's 2013 bankruptcy put the pensions of thousands of retirees at risk. And the vast majority of both private and public pension funds remain severely underfunded today. Yet many pension funds also provide workers with some degree of ownership in their companies. Has this ownership delivered any real power to workers? We asked G. William "Bill" Domhoff, who ranks among the most influential U.S. sociologists, having authored four of the top 50 sociology best-sellers in the past half-century. While many social scientists study the problems of the disadvantaged, Domhoff trains his eye on the wealthy and powerful. He spoke with us about the corporate and political forces driving pension fund capitalism.

Rahsaan Mahadeo: You're famous for writing about the power elite in books like *Who Rules America?* and *The Powers That Be.* Why would someone so interested in power structures shift his focus to pension funds?

Bill Domhoff: Precisely because of my interest in power structures! People were asserting that pension funds were a new way for investors, workers, and so on to really have a significant influence within corporations. Since my research led me to conclude that it is the owners and managers of large corporations—more specifically, their directors and high-level executives—that dominate corporations, I was surprised by this assertion. I also knew that there was a "responsible pension fund" movement, so I decided to look into that more closely.

I soon found that not only do these pension funds not have *any* impact on large corporations beyond very superficial levels, the issue was fascinating in and of itself. The pension fund movement that started in the '80s was, strangely enough, started by a moderate Republican working in the Labor Department in the Reagan administration. His basic motivation was to say that investors should pressure corporations to maximize shareholder value. And that became the shibboleth of the movement. From his point of view, that means that corporations would make maximum payouts. He was soon joined by some pension fund managers who also liked that particular idea, but then it slowly morphed into another dimension: *corporate responsibility*. That is, you're responsible to the shareholders for maximum value, but you are also supposed to be a little bit socially responsible as well. The newspapers picked up on it, and it looked like a bit of a challenge to corporations in the late 1980s and early 1990s.

But, in fact, the Labor Department never implemented any pension fund rules of real significance. And when Republicans took over in the state of California, they changed the Pension Fund Board. They were able to put some pressure on the head of the Pension Fund, who had been hired under Democrats, but he lowered his profile a year or so later, left the Pension Fund, and went into the private sector where he managed some money and sat on the board of a small corporation. So, that was the heart of the movement. It was, in many ways, over by the middle of the 1990s. By then, there were a couple of organizations that were basically pushing for corporate responsibility, and they persisted. They were able to obtain publicity in newspapers like the *New York Times* and in business-oriented magazines, and they were able to present their case to stockholders. *And* they were able to consult for groups that were concerned about trying to control corporations—this included church-based groups, which had started a common organization, "Investors'

Responsibility," a kind of interfaith organization. They also involved unions as well as public kinds of pensions. Even though it's a lot of money between union funds and public pension funds, it still wasn't big enough to have much clout compared to corporate pension funds. The group's successes shrank.

In an attempt to sustain this pension fund movement, this pension fund responsibility group invited corporate pension funds to join. Of course, they did, and soon came to not vote for anything that was very progressive! By the early 2000s, pretty much, these people had given up in frustration. In my article, I quote somebody as saying, in 2000, "We've done all the easy things, and maybe by now we should give up." And by 2004, a couple of people that were leaders had, in fact, gone on to other things. A couple still persist, but it really did fizzle out.

Mahadeo: While all of this began in the 1990s, what are the implications for those who still have their money tied up in pension funds now? What does this mean for the average person?

Domhoff: Well, the people who are recipients of pension funds only really have a right to a certain amount of money. They don't really have control of the pension funds. So I don't think there really is much that they can do; their rights are carefully constricted and there are a lot of laws behind the way pension funds operate. There's a promise of money, but that doesn't mean you have any particular control. And I don't think there's a lot that can be done.

I think this is really symbolized by something I've recently learned from a fine new sociologist, Michael McCarthy, who wrote a dissertation on pension funds in the post-WWII era. And a part of his work concerns the union pension funds, which are partly controlled by either the corporate management or sometimes by what are called "fiduciaries"—finance people who are legally bound to maximize the value of this pension fund and deliver the best that they can to the people who are recipients. McCarthy has found that many, many times, the money of a union pension fund is invested in antiunion corporations! The unions have been able to make a little noise about this, but it's not become exactly a headline story in newspapers. It gives you an idea of how these things can boomerang, when union pension funds are invested in the stocks of antiunion corporations! They're not entirely antiunion corporations—there's a range—but this shows how this money can get away from you as far as issues of power and control (which, since the outset, has been the focus of my work).

Mahadeo: You've also addressed the term *pension fund socialism*. I'm curious as to why you say this is "more rhetoric than reality."

Domhoff: *Pension fund socialism* is a term that came from a management guru, Peter Drucker. He told managers how to do better and how corporations could be great. He claimed that if socialism was defined by ownership of corporations by the workers, my goodness, we have pension fund socialism!

I say it's more "rhetoric than reality" because, of course, these workers did not have any control, really, over these pension funds. Back in the mid-1930s, when both private pensions and pension funds controlled by big corporations were in real trouble in the face of the Great Depression, they weren't getting the returns on their investments, but they had an increasingly large number of retirees. At the same time that the New Deal wanted to create both unemployment insurance and "old age" pension funds, pension operators realized that if they turned their pension funds over to the federal government, it would be cheaper for them. Furthermore, they could then use private pension funds as sort of "icing on the cake" for higher-level executives. By the mid-1930s—way earlier than the political scientists and the sociologists who have written on this realized—pension fund managers were really hip to the fact that they could build a private pension fund scheme on top of Social Security.

WWII then had a dramatic impact on all aspects of American life. During the war, unions were not allowed to bargain much over wages. There were wage-price ceilings (understandably, or else inflation would have run wild), but the National Labor Relations Board ruled that there weren't ceilings on negotiations over side benefits. So, unions began to try to bargain for pension funds, as well as health benefits, since they couldn't get better wages for their workers.

In this context unions were able to get in on the idea of private pension funds, and they did grow a bit, to the consternation of the corporate people. One particular union bargained for its own pension fund that it controlled in the coal industry. And the Teamsters were able to get control of their pension fund, which their leaders promptly—by the '50s—used to finance crooked kinds of ventures, putting money into casinos in Las Vegas and so on.

Curbing the expansion, the 1947 Taft Hartley Act, an important constriction on the rights of unions, said unions couldn't control a pension fund alone. Pensions must be, at minimum, jointly controlled with management. So, at that point, it was hard for unions to ever really have any control over their pension funds. But they fought like the very devil to maintain those private pension funds and health insurance—you know, other little side bennies that were social insurance.

Now, the reason they took that direction is very important in terms of power analysis. That is, the plan by pretty liberal unions had been to try to unionize the southern United States, and they failed. If you can't unionize the South, then you can't possibly have enough liberal Democrats in Congress to create a national health care system or a better pension system. Essentially, the political economy of the South, originally slave based and then low wage, sharecropper based, made it so the unions didn't really have much choice but to bargain for the best possible private pension plans and health insurance they could get. And that went on, of course, into the 1950s and continued, to some extent.

An important limit was that the more money and health insurance you got for your retired workers, the less you were likely to get for your *current* workers. So it created a tension within the unions between those who were currently employed—the young people starting out—and those already retired. At that point, the unions put a tremendous amount of effort into trying to pass

Medicare and did play a very big role in its passage in 1965.

So, that gives you a real sense of the power angles that were going on in public and private pension funds. Corporations in the '30s went for this two-tier kind of thing so they could reward their executives with higher pensions, but lo and behold, WWII allowed unions to force themselves onto the stage. Then unions had to fight very hard (in a context in which they had a real chance to win) in the late '50s over the pensions and they then fought for Medicare, which they won in 1965.

Mahadeo: You mention a lot of the resistance to pension funds that came from growing private companies after WWII, and I'm curious if what you describe as the "rapacious and often illegal actions" of corporate boards indicate similar resistance today. Is this how corporate boards express their disdain for public pension funds?

Domhoff: Well, the interesting thing is that there was one strain within big business—what I call the "corporate moderates"—that continued to be supportive of Social Security throughout the early post-WWII era. They were for changes and improvement—including indexing of Social Security, which means the pension payments go up with inflation—in the early 1970s and in the Nixon administration. By 1980, though, these corporate moderates had turned against the growth of Social Security and thought it was out of hand.

From that point on, they've been pushing the idea that Social Security is going to "break the bank"—that is, it's going to bankrupt the country. I think that's false because, indeed, you could do a number of things, including taxing not only the first $106,000 of income, but the first 1, 5, 10, or 15 million! That would go a long way to solve these alleged "problems."

This scare campaign hasn't been created so much through corporate boards as through think tanks and policy discussion groups. These organizations put out reports about the impending disaster of Social Security. And when we've looked at the boards of these think tanks and policy discussion groups, of course they're the people who are the directors of the major corporations in the United States!

Mahadeo: In your research, you've discussed some of the failures and successes of the California Public Employees Retirement System (CalPERS). What role does government play in pension fund activism at the state and national levels?

Domhoff: Well, I think the state plays the key role—a pivotal role—because the pension fund activists in California, with this plan called CalPERS, were really working with the blessing (the quiet blessing) of the Democratic administration and the treasurer of California, who I think sits on their board. That board is appointed by the Democratic governor (of course, there are some hold-overs from the past, but basically, like with many boards and agencies, they change leadership with changes in administration). So when the Democrats were in office and they had a pretty Democratic state, pension funds were a little more assertive and made a lot of public claims. They would put out reports showing corporations were derelict in one thing or another. The state then played the same kind of role when conservative Republicans came into office, because those administrations clipped the wings of the leadership of CalPERS.

Being in control of government is crucial in all of these things. Basically, in America, we have a corporate conservative coalition that does battle with a liberal labor coalition. That battle happens, first and foremost, in Washington, but it certainly is a battle that went on in major states like California, New York, and others. It was fought in the South, the Great Plains, and many of the Rocky Mountain states, where for a long time to come, the corporate conservative coalition has a lock. The liberal labor coalition has been more dominant, more prominent, in many Northern states. In the last few decades, once-moderate Republicans who held offices and sway in the Northeast and a lot of the Northern states have now been replaced by ultraconservative Republicans. What happens with anything having to do with pensions, with social insurance, depends upon whether the conservatives are dominant (whether they're called Democrats or Republicans) or whether centrist, liberal, labor kinds of people are in power.

PARTICIPANT PROFILE

G. William Domhoff is Distinguished Professor Emeritus and Research Professor at the University of California, Santa Cruz. More information about all of his work can be found on whorulesamerica.net.

old narratives and new realities

KEVIN LEICHT

The simple narrative of who gets ahead in America is in serious trouble. Social scientists know that systems of inequality work best when they generate a coherent narrative about how people get ahead, and this includes fairly elaborate descriptions of who is rewarded for what they do (and who is not rewarded for doing something else). Cultural ideologies are the stories we use when we lack other information. These narratives or ideologies are usually part truth and part fiction, and for many of us they exist at the level of stories that are passed from one generation to another as a sort of "to-do" list for getting ahead.

In the United States, if we're told Mary makes more money than Suzie, we'll assume that Mary works harder than Suzie, has more education than Suzie, or is smarter than Suzie. We *aren't* likely to say that Mary's parents are wealthier than Suzie's, that Mary's social connections are better than Suzie's, or that Mary is just luckier than Suzie. Worse still, if Suzie has the misfortune of being poor, we're more likely to attribute negative characteristics to her to explain the discrepancy (we might, for instance, surmise that Suzie is a drug user). We'll *certainly* assume that Mary is free of these characteristics.

The combined changes in the U.S. political and economic systems over the past 30 years have deprived us of plausible stories that people can use as guidebooks for doing well (or making good). To demonstrate how much things have changed, let's contrast what parents said to their children as late as the 1970s with the way the current system works. These are the shifting rules of the middle-class game, each stemming from the last:

- "Go to a state university and get a good education for a modest price." But tuition goes up every year, and state universities are underfunded. Student loans mean you'll start adulthood in debt.
- "Find a good, steady job. All work is dignified." But good, steady jobs are hard to come by. In an age of celebrity, manual labor is seen as distasteful.
- "Companies reward loyal, hardworking people. You'll get raises and promotions if you work hard." But there are no rewards for loyalty, even if you are able to get and keep that good, steady job.

- "Get married and settle down." But economic uncertainty undermines marriage, and buying a house and paying the mortgage are incredibly hard.
- "Save for a rainy day." But the U.S. savings rate hit zero for the first time in 2006. Effectively, we aren't saving. We can't.
- "You'll retire in your sixties with a gold watch and a pension. Those are your golden years!" But retirement is increasingly an unreachable dream, and company-paid pensions are a thing of the past.

The new reality doesn't describe a coherent narrative for getting ahead. It's just a sad statement of bleak facts. So what's the new advice? "Choose your parents well!" Hmm. Yes, rates of mobility have stagnated and socioeconomic status is largely inherited, but that's not exactly a realistic proposition.

Others might suggest that the problems of old age can simply be eliminated. Unfortunately, this means repackaging old age, not actually addressing problems. Susan Jacoby, Scott Fitzgerald, and I have all noticed that just when Americans can't afford to retire or spend our golden years fishing (we realize you might have other plans), suddenly "60 is the new 30!" Of course it is: Nobody can afford to be old, so they just won't be. They'll work as much or as little as their savings and investments allow, aging into a life span lengthened by medicine but constrained by economics.

Still others might suggest merciless pragmatism. As grandmothers have said the world 'round: "It's as easy to fall in love with a rich man as a poor one." And, sure, college can be a good investment, especially if you pursue a business degree and if the roommate you've been assigned happens to be the next Bill Gates or Mark Zuckerberg.

As you can tell, these ideas are patently absurd. We can't choose our parents or predetermine our social connections or rely on working until we die. These aren't ways forward, just reminders that we are, in many ways, powerless to seek our own American dream.

Many will argue that the same situation is facing young people around the world, but it's not. The U.S. rate of social mobility is among the lowest in the 34 Organisation for Economic Co-operation and Development (OECD) nations. Many countries have rising inequality, but none has inequality numbers that look as daunting as ours. And if we can't come up with a plausible cultural narrative, people will lose faith in the system. Why follow the rules? Why bother with college? Why go to work at a dead-end job? If it's not a step toward something "better," toward a dream, it's hard to see why young people would follow the ladders of an admittedly out-of-date, lockstep notion of life stages.

Clearly something is wrong when chance and luck play a bigger role in who gets ahead than skill and investment. If nothing else, people need to realize that there is no single easy solution, such as getting more education, that will fix the rather understandable malaise afflicting so many of us. Employers, investors, and the global market are capable of treating educated workers as badly as uneducated workers. There is no "personal lifeboat" to get us out of this mess. We can start with reasserting the basic dignity of a job well done, and we can stop championing the "success" of those who gain wealth and power with unearned incomes, paving the way for their children to lead a life of privilege behind them. It's policy, however, rather than pie-in-the-sky hopes that American minds can be changed overnight, that will get us back on track.

Indeed, the rhetorical exercise of trying to sort the old narrative from the new reality makes one thing crystal clear: The economy and its long-term effects on the life course (the markers of age and progression through adulthood) are social problems in need of society-level solutions. We've done it before—lest you forget the Works Progress Administration under the New Deal or the establishment of Social Security or even unionization movements that brought better pay and greater safety to tough but dignified work. Now we just have to do it again.

TSP tie-in

deeper in debt

According to the National Bureau of Economic Research, the Great Recession officially ended in the United States by June 2009. But while financial and housing markets made significant gains in the next five years, the recovery has been *painfully* slow in the United States and much of the world. Even as U.S. stock market indices reached all-time highs in 2014, millennials (those born after 1980) have hardly profited. Scarred deeply by the financial crisis, those who *can* afford to invest seem to be hoarding cash rather than playing in the market—just as life course sociologist Glen Elder observed in 1974's *Children of the Great Depression*. Many more *can't* afford to invest, wracked by student debt, high housing costs, and a persistently difficult labor market.

These generational effects are just one example of the enduring impact of the debt crisis on wealth and inequality. And while the new sociology of debt is well represented in *Owned*, TSP's website is teeming with lively discussions of debt's many facets. To name a few:

- On the 40th anniversary of the Equal Credit Opportunity Act, Lisa Wade of Sociological Images explained how it wasn't until 1974 (!) that women gained the right to have credit cards in their own names.

- In "Bondsy and the Modern Myth of Barter," David Banks of Cyborgology explains a new app that allows you to barter with friends. Banks concludes that "Bondsy affords a new way of looking at commodities' value by reasserting the social nature of objects."

- On Girl w/ Pen, Virginia Rutter highlights new work by Rachel Dwyer (featured in our roundtable), Randy Hodson, and Laura McLeod showing why men are more likely to drop out of college. Their *Gender & Society* article found that female college dropouts face a greater financial penalty than male college dropouts. This important study was also featured in a Reading List item by Kia Heise.

- While student debt is grabbing headlines, Katharine Broton and Sara Goldrick-Rab of the Scholars Strategy Network (SSN) highlight a less discussed but related issue: homelessness and housing instability among college students.

- On our Office Hours podcast, sociologist Lane Kenworthy talks about his new book, *Social Democratic America* (Oxford University Press, 2014), and the current state of American inequality.

- When it comes to deficits and national debt, Benjamin Page finds an enormous class divide in policy preferences.

His SSN brief reports that 53% of all Americans cited jobs as the most important problem, but 87% of wealthy Americans believe the national debt is the most important issue.

While interest in debt was no doubt spurred by the Great Recession, the current spate of research and discussion on the topic will surely outlast the debts themselves. To see these resources and more, check the links at thesocietypages.org/owned.

—RAHSAAN MAHADEO

discussion guide
and group activities

discussion guide

1. While many sociologists focus on the most disadvantaged in society, Kevin Leicht shows how the American middle class has lost ground since the 1970s. How and in what ways did their fortunes decline? Have you or your friends made changes to your lifestyle since the 2008 recession?

2. In "Old Narratives and New Realities," Leicht contrasts what parents told their kids in the 1970s with current realities. What advice have you gotten from friends and mentors?

3. The relationship between debt and inequality is a central theme in *Owned*. Many chapters show how debt is experienced differently depending on our station in life. Visit the thesocietypages.org/owned to read "Too Poor to Go Broke." How are bankruptcy laws

demonstrative of the middle-class squeeze highlighted in this volume?

4. In his chapter, Jason Houle explains why it will be harder for young adults to pay off their debt than earlier generations. In a recent post on Sociological Images, Lisa Wade uses Houle's piece to ask whether accumulating excessive amounts of student debt is simply the gamble most students take when pursuing a college degree. How much risk taking are you or were you willing to do? How do you think economic policy might best accommodate higher-education needs and financial limits?

5. In "Debt and Darkness," David Schalliol describes the struggles of many cities to maintain the basic infrastructure of urban life. Visit our Office Hours podcast to listen to Robert Sampson's interview on "The Neighborhood Effect." What are the connections among debt, crime, and neighborhood effects? What does this have to do with the availability of adequate street lighting?

6. Alexes Harris concludes that the criminal justice system should abolish all monetary sanctions, with the exception of restitution for victims. Browse online to listen to some segments from the 2014 National Public Radio series "Guilty and Charged," particularly those relating to "debt fugitives" and amnesty programs. What fines and fees seem reasonable to you? Would you abolish some court fees and keep others?

7. Our Roundtable on the racial wealth gap begins with an astounding statistic: The average white family has about 10 times the wealth of the average African American family. Why do you think the wealth gap is so much greater than the education gap, the income gap, and the unemployment gap? What policies might reduce these great disparities in wealth?

8. Consider the "debt resistance" movements that Andrew Ross and Erin Hoekstra describe. Under what circumstances is it fair to forgive debts?

9. Among the climate reparations proposals discussed in "Of Carbon and Cash," which seem most appropriate?

10. Why do you think Eric Best emphasizes the debt problems of students at "for-profit" schools when students at public universities face similar problems? Why does he believe fixing the system is going to be so expensive, disruptive, and unpopular?

group activities

ACTIVITY 1: IMAGES OF INEQUALITY

At the intersection of art and sociology, visual sociology explores society and culture through images. In this volume, David Schalliol describes how Detroit's overwhelming debts and great inequality are seen through the absence of streetlights and resulting fear. He also shows us Detroit through a series of stark images, making the contrast between light and darkness come alive.

Visit Schalliol's website (davidschalliol.com) to look through some of his other photography and listen to the Office Hours podcast interview with the "sociophotographer" at thesocietypages.org/owned.

After familiarizing yourself with his work, create your own photo series to depict an aspect of inequality in your community. If Schalliol wanted to highlight inequality in your community, what might he show?

With your discussion group, talk about one another's photo series. What forms of inequality are represented in these images? What visual cues illustrate the presence of inequality? Consider how the statement of an inequality is helped or hindered by a visual representation and how images could help inform and push changes that might alleviate the inequality.

ACTIVITY 2: CONSTRUCT AN ACADEMIC GENOGRAM

In Chapter 5, Robert Crosnoe cites evidence that parents who return to or enroll in college while their children are still in grade school strengthen and promote their kids' academic progress. Based on the example at thesocietypages.org/owned, create a genogram—or "academic family tree"—of your educational lineage. Write your name on the *back* and put it up so that everyone in your discussion group can look at the genograms. What patterns emerge? Reflect on one or all of these questions:

1. How has your academic lineage shaped your experience in higher education?

2. To what extent have you reduced, maintained, or extended your academic lineage?

3. How does parental education seem to affect the educational trajectories of the people in your discussion group?

about the contributors

Eric Best is in the department of emergency management at Jacksonville State University. He is the author, with Joel Best, of *The Student Loan Mess: How Good Intentions Created a Trillion-Dollar Problem* (University of California Press, 2014).

Robert Crosnoe is in the department of sociology and the Population Research Center at the University of Texas at Austin. He is the author of *Fitting In, Standing Out: Navigating the Social Challenges of High School to Get an Education* (Cambridge University Press, 2011).

Alexes Harris is in the sociology department at the University of Washington. She studies social control and how institutions assess, label, and process individuals and groups.

Douglas Hartmann is in the department of sociology at the University of Minnesota. His research interests focus on race and ethnicity, multiculturalism, popular culture (including sports and religion), and contemporary American society. He is coeditor of The Society Pages.

Erin Hoekstra is in the sociology program at the University of Minnesota, where she works on the Flexible Work and Well-Being Project of the Work, Family, and Health Network.

Jason N. Houle is a sociologist and demographer at Dartmouth College. He studies social stratification and mobility, household debt, and health disparities.

Wing Young Huie is an award-winning documentary photographer and author in Minneapolis, Minnesota.

Kevin Leicht is in the department of sociology and is the director of the Iowa Social Science Research Center at the University of Iowa's Public Policy Center. With Scott T. Fitzgerald, he is the author of *Middle Class Meltdown in America: Causes, Consequences, and Remedies* (Routledge, 2014).

Rahsaan Mahadeo is in the sociology program at the University of Minnesota. A former caseworker, he is a Ford Foundation Pre-Doctoral Diversity Fellow.

David Schalliol is in the sociology program at the University of Chicago. He is currently focusing—academically and artistically—on the processes that facilitate social organization and disorganization in urban contexts. He is the author of *Isolated Building Studies* (Utakatado, 2014).

Christopher Uggen is a sociologist and criminologist at the University of Minnesota. He believes that good science can light the way to a more just and safer world. He is coeditor of The Society Pages.

Index

Note: Italicized page locators refer to photos/figures.